The Rock Garden

THE EXCITING VARIETY OF ROCK PLANTS

HERMIEN VAN WIJHE-RUYS

INTRODUCTION BY RICHARD ROSENFELD

 **REBO** PRODUCTIONS

*This book is dedicated to my father, without whose foresight
I would never have ended up at Huis te Lande.*

© 1995 Rebo Productions, Lisse
© 1997 Published by Rebo Productions Ltd
Text: Hermien van Wijhe-Ruys
Design and layout: Ton Wienbelt, The Netherlands
Photo editor: TextCase, The Netherlands
Production: TextCase, The Netherlands
Translation: Andrew May for First Edition Translations Ltd, Great Britain
Typesetting: Hof&Land Typografie, The Netherlands

ISBN 1 901094 45 6

Contents

Foreword

This book is intended as a guide for the novice rock gardener, and is an attempt to outline and explain the different possibilities for growing rock garden plants as clearly as possible. The different types of stone mentioned are not difficult to find. I have limited the discussion of different types of stone, although I realize that there are many more suitable types available. These are, however, scarce and therefore more expensive and difficult to obtain. Fortunately rock gardens are still gaining in popularity, which ensures that the choice of materials, including types of stone, continues to grow. In every garden centre it is possible to choose from a wide selection. Until recently people grew only alpine plants, many of which are difficult to propagate and usually require a greenhouse to grow them successfully. Now people are begining to value the simpler plants, which some growers are bringing on to the market. Whether or not they are associated with a rock garden society, various rock garden enthusiasts are holding regular sales in order to encourage a wider interest in rock gardens. You can find the addresses of various societies at the end of the book.

I am sure that I have not given enough detail about the plants, but I have tried as far as possible to mention plants that are easily available, and are not too difficult to grow. I have consulted the various catalogues from growers given at the back of the book, and also the RHS Plant Finder, which is invaluable. When you look at the catalogues, or visit a specialist nursery you will see that there is a large choice.

I hope that this book will give you many hours of pleasure and that it will make a useful contribution to the pursuit of your hobby.

Opposite page:
Androsace *require very little space.*

Hermien van Wijhe-Ruys

Following page:
Cypripedium regale *is rewarding and easy to grow. It thrives in a fen border.*

Introduction

Rock gardens are coming back in fashion. At the start of the century plant collectors like the Rothschilds at Exbury, near Southampton, created rock gardens that looked just like the real thing. The real thing being a gigantic chunk of the Himalayas. A mini-railway line had to be laid across a cleared forest to shunt in the great slabs of stone weighing several tons apiece for this sunken garden which took four years to excavate, build up, and finish. It's now packed with alpine rhododendrons from China and the Himalayas.

The problem is people think this is the one and only style. As Hermien van Wijhe-Ruys shows, it isn't. Big does not have to be best. And you don't have to grow big plants.

Rock gardens are made for alpines which like getting their anchoring roots into tough, stony, free-draining ground, and they simply hate the damp. You can try a large-scale effect, but frankly it won't work; in the average garden it will look decidedly bizarre and odd. And getting that natural look, with rocks tumbled on rocks, is hard. Far better, and easier, to create something like a hyprtufa tub, and stand it in a yard.

The traditional technique involves making a mould using two strong cardboard boxes, one inside the slightly larger one, which must have several sealed drainage holes at the base.
You then fill the gap with a mix of sand, cement, and sphagnum peat, and water, at the ratio of 1:1:2, and leave to set. Finally, smear over the entire exterior surface with manure and milk, and it will encourage the growth of lichens.

The biggest problem of growing alpines is that you get the collecting bug. A friend of mine has now made 58 small tubs packed with what are known as cushion plants. They are the great survivors. They live on mountainous slopes with rampaging, fierce extremes; snow, winds, and sun. That's partly why they are usually dome-shaped. Under the surface there's usually last year's dead foliage, which makes a kind of tough, resilient springy surface so falling rocks and sweeping-down packs of snow roll over them. The plants also have penetrating, anchoring roots to hang on. And out of this incredible will to survive comes fabulous mounds of flowers.

Edraiathus pumilio comes from the Dalmation Mountains, and was once famously described by the English plant hunter Reginald Farrer (1880-1920, and author of the classic
2-volume book *The English Rock Garden)* as "the jewel of the family… built of spiny, glistening, pointed little leaves, with their upper surfaces coated in silvery, closeplied silk." Which may be a tad over the top, but it shows how cushion plants grab you, and try to become an obsession. And the effect of gardening in miniature, bending each day over a hand-size clump of foliage, waiting, waiting, waiting, until what in the wild hangs onto the most wretched surfaces, gently opens its flowers.

Hermien van Wijhe-Ruys covers all kinds of plants for the rock garden, not just the cushion kind. There are ferns and bulbs, saxifrage and geraniums, even the spectacular *Calceolaria darwinii*, which looks like a very bizarre orchid, with yellow flowers and a freckled yellow lip, and a white band between pouch and throat. It is, if you like, a splendid book of a menu. Order fast, get growing, and don't be surprised if you become a fanatic.

Richard Rosenfeld, East Sussex, 1996

More about rock plants

In this chapter, the natural habitat of these beautiful, delicate plants with their brightly coloured flowers will be discussed in some detail.

Origanum scabrum

The origins of rock plants

Before starting with the construction of a rock garden, it is worth pausing to consider the nature of rock plants and where they actually originated. Plants that grow high up in the mountains used to be called rock plants and are often referred to as "alpine" plants. More recently many "normal" plants that flourish in the rock garden are referred to as rock plants.

Mountain vegetation

In the mountains you find alpine plants in the zone between the forests and the permanent snow (also known as the snow-line) or on bare rock. They are low-growing plants that cluster in tightly packed carpets. They grow under extreme conditions, especially in harsh winters with storm force winds and temperatures far below freezing, and where the summer is brief. Plants that are able to grow here have adapted themselves to withstand these extreme conditions. Although the temperatures are so low, there is usually a layer of snow that offers the plants some protection. The reason that plants often freeze in our environment is not because of the cold, but because they are uncovered. Snow is an ideal insulator. Typically all the plant growth above the ground dies off, but as soon as the snow has melted, the roots revive and the plant is green again in no time.

In mountainous regions there are different zones or belts. The number of zones depends on the altitude of the region. The foothills extend to about 600m (1,969ft). The alpine zone is the area between 600m and

1400m (1,969ft and 4,593ft). In this zone there are deciduous and mixed forests, as in the upper regions of the medium-sized mountain ranges such as the Alps, Pyrenees, and Carpathians.

Above the deciduous belt there is a subalpine belt that extends from 1400m (4,593ft) as far as the tree line.

The tree line is between 1800m and 2200m (5,906ft-7,218ft).

In central Europe the alpine zone extends to about 3000m (9,843ft). This zone is the area with mountain meadows and bare rock.

The woody plants of this region are the so-called "creeping" trees and shrubs. They grow with their branches close to the ground.

The brilliantly coloured alpine cushion or mat-forming plants, that are usually no taller than 10cm (4in), grow in the mountain meadows and on screeslopes. Many of these plants are also found in the arctic regions, specifically in the mountain tundra. A few of these plants are in fact circumpolar, meaning that they grow throughout the polar regions.

Plants do not grow at the same altitude all over the world. In warmer regions, such as the mountains in east Africa, plants still grow at about 5000m (16,404ft).

In Indonesia and Malaysia, as well as the Himalayas, there are still various types of azalea to be found at 4000m (13,123ft). The nice thing about this is that the plants do not reflect their harsh surroundings. The higher, the prettier is often true.

Snow is like a blanket for the plants.

9

Birds and insects are attracted to the bright colour and sweet perfume of Daphne cneorum *'Variegata'*

It is amazing that as soon as the snow has melted, the beautifully coloured *Soldanella* displays its loveliest features at a height of about 3000m (9,843ft). The *Potentilla*, a member of the rose family, is still found at an altitude of 3300m (10,827ft) in rocky, mountain meadows.

Similarly, at about 3300m to 3400m (10,827ft-11,155ft), *Leontopodium*, the edelweiss and *Antennaria* still manage to survive on grassy hills.

It has already been pointed out that these plants have adapted to the inclement weather conditions. Pieces of rock are easily lifted up by the wind and can land on the plants. The plants often resemble cushions, because they are better protected from the harsh conditions if they are close-growing. Often the cushions are so small that you have to lie face down in order to see them.

Alpine plants are also adapted to their environment in other ways. Any plants with strong, brittle twigs would have them broken off, so the stems have to be flexible. The shrubs that grow at the highest altitudes have prostrate stems and leaves.

The willow trees whose habitat is the damp hills from 1600m to 3000m (5,249ft-9,843ft) are obvious examples of prostrate shrubs. With *Salix reticulata* and *S. herbacea*, the catkins are often found in the leaf axils. There are also hardy plants with a similar growth habit. From a distance it looks as if they are mosses, but as you approach,

Leontopodium alpinum *ssp.* nivale *recalls the mountains. It remains smaller than other members of this species.*

these mosses reveal themselves to be higher plants. In the high mountainous regions, the *Silene* displays its true self on a sunny day, when the pink flowers open. Then there is no mistaking it for a clump of moss.

Plants can grow even in the narrowest of crevices. Sometimes they are so tiny that you need a practised eye to discover them.

These plants, which are also called cliff or abyss plants or chasmophytes, usually grow singly in isolation, safely hidden from grazing animals and greedy human hands. Obviously they find sufficient food and water to survive there. Various members of the pink family *(Caryophyllaceae)* are also perfectly able to live in such a habitat.

Subtropical rock plants

So far I have only talked about plants that grow among snow and ice. There are, however, tropical and subtropical rock plants. In Great Britain there are whole groups of subtropical plants, including *Aloe*, *Agapanthus* and *Agave*, which can grow on rock, and flower freely there in the milder parts of the country.

Cyclamen coum *blooms abundantly in February.*

Following pages: The 'natural' rock garden is the most beautiful.

11

Building the rock garden

Naturally it all depends on the available space and the position of your rock garden. You don't necessarily have to put rock plants in a rock garden; rock plants feel equally at home on walls, in gravel beds, and elsewhere.

Androsace *is very suitable for rock crevices.*

At first it will cost you a good deal of effort, but once you are simply keeping up with the maintenance of your garden, you will realize that well-thought-out planning and a thorough preparation give the most pleasure. Even though public rock gardens are usually extensive, you can come across many ideas in such gardens. Go and visit them particularly to see which plants are used and how they grow in relation to the sun.

Conditions

Sun and protection

Most rock plants require a lot of sunlight and like to bask in the sun. However, there are some varieties that can survive in the shade, as long as they are not in the shadow of overhanging branches. It is better not to build a rock garden in a wooded area. You can quickly create something more attractive there with a selection of shade-loving plants plants for ground cover.

When you decide to build a true rock garden, it is better to choose an open aspect.
In their natural surrounding rock plants always have more than enough sun. A south-facing position is ideal. If possible shelter them from northerly and westerly winds. Rock plants usually have to tolerate harsh conditions in the mountains, but during the winter they are hidden under a thick layer of snow which can provide the necessary protection.

Your surroundings   If you live in an area where sloping ground is the exception, it can be difficult to create a natural-looking rock garden. Of course there are places where the landscape is hilly and where there are loose rocks. Such places offer ideal opportunities for building a rock garden.

But even if you live in a flat landscape such as the Fens in East Anglia, there are enough opportunities to establish a rock garden.

Then you have to search for a suitable backdrop against which you can design your garden. And of course it is possible to make a mound in the garden.

You can also let a rock garden form a transition to a bog or heather garden.

Using a hill as the basis   A good background for a rock garden is a group of shrubs that is planted to look as if there are mountains in the distance. Against this type of background you can create a beautiful garden.

Dig the ground out just in front of the shrubs so that there is enough room to create a natural-looking slope.

Make the slope with the excavated earth. Do not make the slope too regular; ridges and crevices look better. If you leave bits open here and there, a rock garden looks very natural.

You have no doubt realised that such a rock garden will need a considerable area of ground.

A rock garden will be interesting if shade-loving as well as sun-loving plants can grow in it, as in this garden where every rock face is planted.

Preparatory work   As I have already mentioned, it is essential to ensure very good drainage and good soil.

For rock plants, good soil is actually less important than the right position. A sun-loving plant that is growing in good soil, but in a well-shaded spot, will eventually die off.

A good rock garden must also look natural. If possible, use rocks that fit in with the landscape. Luckily a rock garden still offers plenty of scope for your own creativity.

You can plant like this in among rocks.

Left:
In Prague's botanic garden you can admire this trough with tufa.

Eradicating weeds   Before you even lay the first rock, make sure that the ground is totally free of weeds. If you do not do this beforehand, your rock garden will demand lots of maintenance later. Dig up all the runners or use a systemic weed killer in those places where the weeds are particularly well established.

Heavy soil   As already mentioned, it is important that you mix lots of rubble into heavy soil.

Heavy soil is not very permeable and most rock plants prefer well-drained ground.

Layout When you have satisfied those conditions, you can begin with construction. Wear gloves while you are building your rock garden, even in warm weather, because you can cut yourself badly on sharp pieces of rock. Even safety boots are not a luxury because rubber boots will not protect you against rock, and in clogs you can slip. Although you can start building your rock garden in any season, it is probably better to do this in dry weather. If the rocks are wet then you can easily slip. Begin by digging out the ground in order to make a slope.
Always make sure that the excavated area is slightly larger than the planned rock garden. Keep your design as simple as possible.
A complicated rock garden is not so effective. It certainly cannot do any harm to step back now and again to see how the garden will look as a whole.

The design Excavate the ground according to your plans. You can, for example, make a hollow valley so that the slopes that are filled with rocks and plants open out into a footpath.
You can choose whether you locate the path on a north-south axis, giving both slopes an equal share of sunlight, or from east to west, giving a south-facing slope.
On this slope you can place warmth-loving plants. On the opposite bank you could, for example, plant cushion saxifrages, which do not like direct sun.

The hybrids of Lewisia cotyledon *are beautiful, evergreen plants with lovely pink flowers.*

Instead of a valley, you can also make the banks of your mound slope down to a pond. A pond like that can, to begin with, serve as a reservoir for excess rainwater.

The additional advantage is that in a warm summer, the evaporating water provides cooling and a higher humidity around the plants in the rock garden. A water feature also gives you more possibilities for other plants. With water you attract more birds who love to bathe there. Along with frogs and toads, they ensure that harmful insects will not have a chance in your garden.

You can also make a hillock in one corner of the garden, leading up to a backdrop of shrubs.

Positioning the rocks

In their natural surrounding, layers of rock are usually at least partly covered with soil. Try to imitate this in your garden by placing the largest surface of the rock uppermost.

The most weathered side of the rock is the most attractive. Make sure that the rocks are firmly set in the ground and that they are at a slight angle. Apart from being safer, this means that plants can benefit from the water that is channelled to the soil by the slope of the rocks. If you place the rocks upright the water can run straight off them and your garden will soon dry out.

Only use rocks that you can lift on your own, and start building from the bottom of the slope. Each layer of rock forms the basis for the next

Crocus speciosus *is planted in the autumn.*

layer above it. If the first layer of rocks is firmly placed, you can begin with the second layer.

You carry on building until you reach the desired height. The upper 30cm (12in) of the rock garden must be very well drained. Add rubble, volcanic rock, or gravel.

You will achieve a more natural effect if you use various sizes of rock. Leave big gaps between the rocks, where you can put the soil so that the plants can grow there later.

The gaps must be large enough to allow the plants sufficient room. While you are building the rock garden, you can build-in the crevices where the upright plants will grow.

Planting during construction

Lewisia, *Ramonda*, *Physoplexis*, and *Haberlea* are some of the plants which prefer to grow vertically. There are other plants that you can put in crevices, such as *Erigeron karvinskianum*, *Aubrieta deltoidea*, *Saponaria ocymoides*, *Sedum acre*, and *Silene maritima*. You can plant these during construction. Fill the rock crevices with a well-drained compost rather than garden soil. Garden soil is not suitable for many alpines and some soils are almost impossible to moisten once they have dried out. Push the plants into the damp compost without compacting it. If you have to compress the planting medium then the crevice is too narrow, but as the garden is still under construction, you can simply widen the gap.

The pond in this rock garden attracts many birds.

To prevent the soil being washed out of the crevice, place a stone at the crevice head.

Dianthus alpinus *'Joan's Blood' is most at home in lime-rich soil.*

Learning from experience

As an experienced gardener, it is often difficult to describe the necessary techniques in a book, so I asked a new rock-garden enthusiast to describe her experiences.

After reading her account you will see that laying out a rock garden is easier than you might have thought:

"We started our rock garden in spring 1990.

There was already a little corner with some stones collected from here and there and some rock plants, but it wasn't anything like a real rock garden.

Initially there was a long, narrow garden behind the house, and then a rectangular piece of ground became available to the side of the house which was suitable for laying out a rock garden.

The position of the garden was fixed. Now we had to buy natural stone. We thought that the prices at the garden centres were far too high for our budget so we looked for an alternative. My husband, who had worked as a barge hand, remembered that he had transported natural stone from Engis, in the vicinity of Luik.

So one day, we drove to Belgium to see if we could get any natural stone. After some searching we found a quarry in Engis which sells natural stone retail.

We knew someone who would collect the load of rocks for a reasonable price, and one day a truck tipped 32 tonnes of rock outside our house. An enormous heap of rocks was just lying there in the street. Two things ran through my mind: 'What am I doing?' and 'How do I get all this off the street?' It was quite a job, but with the help of various muscular friends and family members the task was completed in four days. At least, the rocks were behind the house and we could start construction.

The fixed points were a natural pond behind the rock-garden, a stream which was to run from another part of the garden via the rock-garden into the pond, and various paths. Because we didn't think that 1m (3ft) high boulders would be suitable for our garden, we chose smaller variations in height.

From the lowered seating area that we already had behind the pond, where the water level is 1.5m (5ft) below the level of the garden, you get the impression that the differences in height are considerable.

We started building up the rock garden from the edge of the pond. I would sit in the seating area because it was the best place to see how the rocks should be placed. My husband would position the rocks on the other side of the pond, turning each of them round a couple of times, of course. We began with steps running down to the water, and from the water level we worked our way back up.

Each rock was examined and positioned individually. It's very tricky

Ramonda nathaliae is an excellent plant for crevices and cracks.

The plants blend into the rocks.

21

Saponaria and Cory-
dalis *grow abundantly
on this wall.*

to plan a rock garden in advance because no two rocks are alike, and the shape of the beds and the course of the water emerges while you are working. We made some mistakes, of course.

One was that we didn't use enough rubble under the rock. We didn't think it was necessary because our garden has well-drained, permeable soil. That was obviously a mistake. Rock plants like very good drainage as much as they like to bury their roots in rubble.

Now whenever there is the opportunity, we put as much rubble under the rocks as we can.

This type of garden always keeps you busy, experimenting with different things. It's a lovely hobby and trying out the more difficult species in a rock garden is a satisfying challenge."

***Materials for the
rock garden***

More and more often we see the use of rocks, pieces of marble or beautiful random boulders in gardens, whether they are rock gardens or not. Several towns and villages have large free-standing rocks or boulders that are recognisable as landmarks. Think, for example, of the boulder at Amersfoort. In many places in other countries there are boulders, often brought by the ice, which have been used as features in parks. Nowadays you see them more often in private gardens.

An upright piece of slate can accentuate a garden design, while decorative rocks can give a garden a Japanese atmosphere.

Maintenance will be easier if you place a number of cushion saxifages next to each other.

In the Netherlands, natural stone is only found in Limburg, where a soft limestone is quarried. Other material has to be imported from abroad. So there are few Dutch people with a rock garden, but the numbers are increasing. Garden centres are selling more and better materials. The choice of materials depends on taste as well as whether the material is suitable for a rock garden.

Through centuries of exposure to the forces of nature, particularly the water from rivers and mountain streams, rocks acquire their individual forms and structures. Some types of rock are so hard that you can better use these for something else.

Countries such as Great Britain are more fortunate in having many different rocks available.

There are people who claim that rock gardens should consist of only one kind of stone. I do not agree. I have seen gardens where really beautiful effects have been achieved with several kinds together.

Types of rock   Limestone is a pale yellow, or whitish stone, depending on which geological formation it comes from. It used to be popular for rock gardens in Britain and it is, of course, very suitable for lime-loving plants. Unfortunately some limestones are under threat in their natural area, especially the water-worn rocks of the Pennines. For reasons of conservation they should not be used unless the rock is second-hand.

Dryas octopetala in full bloom.

23

The various sandstones available in Britain, which vary in colour according to the area they come from, are very suitable for rock gardens. The natural layers can be imitated in a garden, with stones set at an angle to the slope.

Tufa is ideal stone for the rock-garden. It is formed by the process of deposition. In streams rich in lime, thin layers of calcium carbonate, at most 1mm (1/20in) thick, are deposited on the leaves, pine needles, reeds, weeds, moss, and other debris.

This organic material eventually decays and the lime skeletons remain. This process takes years, and the thick layer of skeletons eventually forms tufa. Tufa can be used indoors and out for lime-loving plants.

To start with it is a rather yellow, but it soon turns grey. You can create a very natural look with tufa because it is so easy to work. You can plant the rock-plants directly in the tufa by first drilling holes in it and filling them with a little soil.

Other plants will seed themselves in it. You can also use tufa as a water channel by drilling holes in it and connecting the underside to a water pump. Look out for good quality material because the softer stone disintegrates easily and this can spoil the whole effect of your rock-garden design.

Tufa is especially attractive when it is used on a slope. Unfortunately it is rather expensive.

It is more attractive to use an igneous rock such as basalt in combination with other kinds of stone. It is a dark, rather sombre-looking rock that was once molten so it has no layered structure.

Some volcanic rocks are useful for alpines because of the cavities. Pumice is a light material that can be shaped easily. This stone is also quite porous and contains little cavities where plants can nestle.

Cultivated plants flourish in it, but unfortunately weeds also try to acquire a stronghold on it. Keep an eye on weeds because it is quite difficult to remove them from the cavities.

Other igneous rocks such as granite, which can be predominantly pink or grey in colour, do not look right in an area away from the mountains. They can also detract from the beauty of the plants because of their bright colour.

A cheap alternative for a garden is slag, a by-product of steel-making foundries. I have used it successfully myself. Slag is mostly used for paths or in chips for the base of tarmac roads, but it can be used in a rock-garden because it is light, porous and easy to lay. Plants do well on it.

River boulders are solid rocks that are carried along by water. They are unsuitable for plants because they do not absorb water. Furthermore, plants cannot usually attach themselves to these stones because they tend to be very smooth.

They are appropriate for a moraine garden. They are found in various

Gentiana sino-odorata *is a beautiful peat-bed plant.*

colours, from white-veined to greyish brown. Look out for interesting shapes and colours.

Boulders from glacial moraine have similar properties to the river boulders. You can make a water course or river bed with these stones, or use them as a filling in between other rocks.

Flagstones have been used in the garden for a long time, mainly for paths and terraces. There are regular and irregular shapes which can be a brilliant foundation for rock plants that grow in the gaps between them. In addition, they are very suitable as stepping stones.

There are also flagstones in other colours, depending on their origin. You can also use these slabs to build a stone wall, with or without mortar.

Thicker blocks can be obtained in the same colour as the flagstones, and they are less breakable. They are very suitable for making a raised bed. Granite blocks are usually used as steps for the rock garden, while granite sets are used for paving.

Paving stones and concrete slabs made with aggregate can be broken in two and used for building a wall.

They are also good for paved gardens, not least because of their low cost. If you find a rock-garden too "rocky" but you would still like to do your gardening from a paved area, you could lay cobblestones.

This type of garden could be called a patio garden instead of a rock garden. Here you can use taller, hardy plants, and shrubs.

A splendid, natural-looking rock-garden.

Split boulders are suitable for paved gardens too. These rocks are too hard and absorb too little moisture to make them suitable for plants. However, plants flourish between the paving stones.

There are many beautiful types of rock. You could also go abroad to see what is available there.

There are often very different materials on sale. If you decide to create a rock-garden which is different from everyone elses, you will have to look elsewhere.

This example of layered limestone is a good example of what can be done.

Planting the rock garden

Just as with "normal" plants, there are sun-loving rock plants as well as plants which flourish well without sunlight, or do even better if they are in the shade. Before you start planting, it is sensible to find out which plants to consider for a sunny position.

Think about bulbous plants and conifers, or other evergreen shrubs, as well as the hardy perennials. These plants ensure some colour in the winter. Sketch on paper approximately where you want to put the plants. It need not be a very detailed plan, but if you have an overall idea, you can take another look to check if the right plants are in the right place and whether you have planned to put in too much.

Remember to consider how much room a plant will need while it is growing. When you buy the plants they are still very small, but they have to be able to spread out. If you have a well thought out scheme, then you can start planting.

Begin with a framework of shrubs and conifers that will also provide some colour in the winter. It is attractive to make a composition with a few upright conifers to contrast with a bushy shape, or combine a nice, rounded shrub with one that has trailing branches that will spill over the rocks like a waterfall.

Nothing looks worse than a rainy, grey, winter day in a garden where there is nothing to catch the eye.

Calceolaria (biflora) is a favourite with aphids.

Now for the planting

For every plant you have to make a generous hollow and fill it with garden soil mixed with sand and peat. One absolute rule is that the plant should stand as deep as it stood in the ground or the pot.

If the roots of a pot-grown plant have come through the bottom of the pot, you have to loosen them carefully and try to damage them as little as possible. Never rip them off. You could possibly cut them off.

The more the roots are damaged, the more difficult it is for the plant to take after transplanting. A young plant with a less established root system will spring fewer surprises than an older plant, because with the younger plant the clump of roots is still relatively small and the green shoots are not yet fully grown, and so it will be more resilient than an older specimen.

It is best to flatten the ball of earth before placing the plant in the ground. Once the plant is in position, fill the rest of the hole with the soil mixture I described above, and press it all down firmly.

TIP

Plants with grey, hairy foliage do not flourish in our humid climate.
Put them in a place where their leaves will stay dry, for example next to the house under the edge of an over-hanging roof.
You can also cover them with a sheet of glass if it rains heavily.

28

If the plant prefers chalky soil, you can mix crushed chalk into the soil. Once you have finished planting, scatter a thin layer of gravel over the surface and then water all the plants.

During dry periods you can water the plants regularly as well; they still have to grow.

Acantholimon arme-mum has beautiful seed capsules.

The planting season   Now that plants are sold in containers, you can actually plant throughout the year, except when there is snow on the ground. For plants that are standing in the open at the nursery, it is best to keep to the usual season for planting. I still use the old-fashioned rules because in the summer you have to take much more care, certainly with sandy soil. A plant is parched in no time. If you plant in the spring or autumn, the chances of it dehydrating are much smaller. Deciduous shrubs and trees are transplanted after they lose their leaves and before the frost sets in. Then it is best not to plant them until they come into bud in the spring. Evergreen shrubs are planted in April or September.

Bury spring-flowering bulbs in the autumn, for example in September, and autumn-flowering bulbs in the spring.

Give woody rock-plants the chance to become established properly before the winter sets in. In other words, plant them in the spring, summer or very early autumn. If there is then a very frosty winter, the roots are already so well developed that they have more resistance to

T I P

Plants with grey foliage like a warm position. Plant them as high as possible in the rock garden.

T I P

Transplant snowdrops
when they are still in
bloom. They will take
better.

the cold which could freeze the plants. They also find it difficult to become established in wet ground, so place them in reasonably dry soil.

If the framework is complete, you can plant the hardy plants. Here you can give your imagination free rein in order to create a striking scene. Remember to look at the sketches where you have noted how much space each plant requires.

Remember that they have to be able to stand up to the competition of their neighbours as well.

Also consider the sun's position and the desired height in the garden. A plant which needs more water prefers a position at the base of the rock garden, while a grey-leafed plant prefers to stand a bit higher.

All these points come up again while you are planting.

Even if you made a good plan, it's useful to position the plants in their place before you finally plant them.

Then you can still change things. Of course you can do this afterwards, but with more effort. Take the growth habit of the plant into consideration. Often the shape of the plant is a good indication of how best to position it.

Pay attention to variety, just as you would in the border. It is not very attractive if one side is filled completely with cushion plants and the other with trailing plants.

You can do anything with Ramonda *so long as you plant it in the shade.*

Alternatives with rock plants

It is not always possible to construct a rock garden: you may have to contend with a lack of space or to work in a garden which is not in the ideal location. Nonetheless, that should not prevent you from working with rock plants.

You can make a column with granite posts and fill it in with tufa.

Rock plants are not solely for use in a rock garden; they also feel perfectly at home on walls and in gravel beds.

Planting on walls or in gravel beds may demand a great deal of effort, but you will find it very enjoyable if you start with a well-thought-out plan and the right preparation. In this chapter I will give you some detailed examples.

Alternative designs and elements

The architectural rock garden

If you think that your town garden is not suitable for a natural rock garden then you might consider constructing an architectural or geometric garden.

This means you must make straight-lined designs on paper beforehand. Although you must eventually work with differences in height for an architectural garden, start working with rectangular stones and blocks – for example, blocks of granite, dressed stone, rectangular flagstones, and so on – instead of stones with irregular shapes.

A rectangular pond or a seating area are well suited to this kind of design. You can use just as many plants in this formal setting as you would in a natural rock garden, siting them on raised beds alternating with terraces, paths, and steps.

You can make a raised bed surrounded with a small supporting wall using the earth excavated from your pond. All kinds of plants can be placed in and on this wall. Think, for example of *Aubrieta*, *Arabis*, *Cerastium*, *Cynbalaria muralis*, and *Iberis*.

This wall can be built from natural stone or bricks; it all depends on your tastes and what is suitable in the setting of your house. Make sure your foundations are firm when you are building this type of wall. Dig a trench 30-40cm (12-16in) deep, depending on the type of ground in your garden. Start at the base with a layer of broken rock which you ram down thoroughly, then put a layer of used bricks bound with mortar. Lay the bricks on top of this foundation.

If you use natural stone then choose attractive stones which are not too large – you can buy these in any good garden centre. Make sure that the wall tapers slightly backwards – about 10cm (4in) for a low wall, and 20cm (8in) for a wall up to 1m (3ft) high. It is hardly necessary to point out that you have to build this kind of wall with due care. Set the prettiest plants in the upper section of the wall.

At first the plants will droop down but once they are firmly rooted they will grow in all directions. Do not make the holes for the plants too large. It is nice when you put the plants in an irregular pattern to avoid monotony; three here and five there.

Do not cover the whole wall but leave some areas bare because it should not look overcrowded. The harmony of colours on a wall is not so important as in a border, especially since the area of wall which you cover with rock plants is never as large as in borders.

On the sunny side of the wall you can plant *Acantholimon, Aster alpinus, Campanula carpatica* and *C. cochlearifolia, Dianthus*

Water in some form or other is indispensable, especially for plants which require plenty of moisture in the growing season.

gratianopolitanus, Onosma, Saponaria ocymoides, and *Sedum acre*. On the shaded side you can grow *Arenaria balearica, Asplenium trichomanes, Haberlea rhodopensis, Corydalis lutea* and *Ramonda*, among others.

An attractive effect has created out of wood.

A rock garden pond

In discussing the construction of a rock garden pond I assume that the pond is going to be lined.

Liner is a relatively cheap material which you can mould to any shape and size of pond. Do not use the cheapest kind because there are large variations in quality.

The liner must be robust because there is nothing worse than a pond springing a leak after such hard work.

There is liner strengthened with fibres which works really well. It is 5mm (1/5in) thick and is available on rolls in widths of 4, 5, 6, and 8m (13, 16, 20, and 26ft).

Add a further 1.5m (5ft) to the planned length and breadth of your pond. Use a garden hose or a length of rope to outline the shape of your pond so that you can find out whether it is to your liking. The more straightforward the shape, the cheaper and easier construction will be.

Position the pond where it will be in the sun for at least 5 hours per day. If it is in the sun all day, you can shade it with hardy perennials and shrubs as well as grasses and groups of water lilies.

Thymus serpyllum is a popular terrace plant.

33

Constructing the pond

First mark the shape and the deep-water area of the pond with small stakes. Now you can start digging.

You can do this by hand if the pond is not so big, otherwise you can rent a mechanical digger or excavator. This will do half the work for you. Use the excavated soil to build up raised sections and slopes in your rock garden. When you have finished digging it is important to check the rim of the pond: it must be level all the way around.

If this is not the case, you must make sure that you make the rim perfectly horizontal using a spirit-level. You can usually correct the level by adding or removing soil.

Complete the walls and the bottom of the pond with a 5cm (2in) layer of builders' sand, peat, or even old carpets and newspapers, then fit the lining. When it is roughly in position you can slowly fill the pond with water.

The liner will now adopt the shape of the pond as the weight of the water presses the liner against the sides and bottom. You can smooth out any possible creases by hand. Attach the liner so that the sides stick out to prevent the water seeping out into the garden.

Previous page: Calceolaria darwinii flowers better in an alpine house than in the open.

It is sensible to strengthen any banks which will be used as walkways. You can do this with stones, but round pieces of wood or even railway sleepers are very suitable.

To avoid damaging the pond liner you should pad the stones or any other hard material with cloth before stretching the liner over them.

Dodecathon meadia loves moisture.

Also construct a small wooden gangway so that any animals venturing into the pond will not be trapped, and drown.

There are also examples of raised beds at Wisley.

During the construction it is wise to think about an electricity point and any tap or hose point.

These are much easier to plan and install to begin with. When you are finished it is much more difficult, and it can make a mess of everything. You have decided that you do not want a water pump now but you might change your mind later on.

Lay your plants loose on top of the ground before beginning planting so that you can change their position if need be. Later on that can still be done, but it will take much more work. Bear in mind the eventual size of the plants.

Usually the shape of the plants is the best indication of the most appropriate position for them.

Make sure that there is plenty of variation just as you would with a border. It is not very attractive if you just have flat flower heads on the one side and straggling plants on the other. Plants that flourish at the side of a pond include *Dodecatheon meadia*, *Iris sanguinea*, *Primula*, *Dactylorhiza*, and *Genista lydia*.

The terrace The terrace offers you the opportunity for some experimentation. With some beautiful rock plants you can transform a monotonous

37

terrace into a colourful pattern of lovely flowers and green cushions. Bear in mind that there are only a few plants which can tolerate repeated scuffing and trampling. You can use all kinds of tiles and paving for your terrace, according to your taste.

You can leave empty spaces in different shapes for siting rock plants or even low-growing shrubs and conifers. You can also allow the plants to seed themselves among the slabs. If you use large paving blocks with a somewhat rough surface, the plants will camouflage the straight lines by spreading out on top of them. This creates a lovely contrast between man-made lines and the natural pattern. This type of composition can – also be achieved with plants growing between the paving stones.

Intertwining thyme and rock carnations can be used to decorate the terrace like this.

Do not try to combine thyme with *Sedum* in the same way, because it will turn out to be a disappointment – *Sedum* will smother the thyme completely.

You can also cover the terrace in *Acaena*, *Antennaria*, *Arenaria*, *Armeria*, *Iberis*, heather, and saxifrage, as well as winter aconite, crocusses, and snowdrops for the early spring.

If necessary, you can fill up the terrace with creeping *Cotoneaster*, a low-growing *Berberis*, and a dwarf rose with its beautiful rosehips – they will make your terrace colourful for a long time.

Lewisia *likes acid soil but flourishes on walls as well.*

You can also work with rock plants on the slabs as well as between them. By putting troughs, containers, and pots on your terrace you can also enjoy the colour and beauty of rock plants from the comfort of your sitting room.

Rock plants instead of grass

It is much more difficult to manage to cultivate rock plants in the space that you had in mind for your lawn.

Chamaemelum nobile 'Treneague' and *Thymus serpyllum* are the most commonly used plants, but you can also try out *Antennaria dioica*.

Unfortunately a lawn consisting of rock plants requires lots of maintenance.

The weeds and the grasses that poke their heads up here and there have to be removed carefully, and even then you will notice that you have to weed them out again every couple of years.

An alpine meadow

The alpine meadow strongly resembles the lawn with rock plants. The difference is that there are grasses in the alpine meadow.

You are almost certainly familiar with them, the meadows high in the mountains which are studded with small, bright, flowering plants.

To create an alpine meadow sow a seed mixture of wild alpines, which will produce as many grasses as perennials. It is very difficult to maintain a good balance between grasses and sedges and the broad-

Arenaria tetraquetra var. gratanensis *can grow between rocks in a very warm position in the rock garden.*

Phlox, Onosma, and Lithodora compliment each other very well.

leafed plants. The plants which you could perhaps grow in the alpine meadow include *Genista sagittalis*, *Helianthemum* 'Wisley Pink', *Dactylorhiza*, *Sagina*, *gentians*, and *thyme*.

A well-designed pond is a visual treat in the rock garden.

Dry stone walls

These walls are particularly suitable for the so-called crevice plants as long as they are not free-standing.

The walls are kept cool by the earth behind them and plants can grow well, especially the ones which are planted in the wall as it is being built.

You can, however, put in the plants after the wall is built. This requires more patience.

The name "dry" indicates that there is no morter used in the wall, but you do have to make a foundation. You dig a trench, which has to be deeper on light soil than on more solid ground, which you fill with a layer of rubble.

You make a layer of stones on top of this, making sure you have a wide foundation, and then you can begin stacking the stones. It is also advisable to build the wall leaning slightly backwards: building up the stones is an art in itself.

You can use the wonderful English walls as an example or you can use a much more personal approach.

Recently I saw paving slabs, broken in half, stacked up with the broken face on display.

There was no cement involved. I thought it was a fantastic idea to grow rock plants on it. In the gaps between the stones on the south-facing side you can place *Lewisia*, *Saxifraga longifolia*, and *Sempervivum montanum*, while on the shaded side you can consider *Cymbalaria muralis*, *Pratia pedunculata*, *Ramonda*, and *Haberlea*.

You can also try to grow plants on a free-standing wall, but experience has shown that you should limit yourself to a small selection – small ferns, *Sedum*, and *Sempervivum tectorum* (the common houseleek) are plants which are happy with very little soil.

A raised bed   It can be fun to make a raised bed, and in this case to grow rock plants in it. A bed is easy to arrange and maintain.

In addition it is much cheaper and it takes up less space to assemble a collection of beautiful, flowering rock plants.

That is why this method of gardening is becoming increasingly popular.

The height of a bed can vary from 30-80cm (12-32in), built between two parallel walls.

It offers a world of possibilities for the enthusiast, who can use it to bring together many small plants in a limited space – *Helianthemum*, *Aubrieta*, *Dianthus*, in fact you can grow anything you want in a raised bed.

A glazed earthenware trough can also be used for rock plants.

A peat bed   The peat bed has come to us from Scotland. It was created by Scottish gardeners in the 1950s, and used as a model for the wonderful botanic gardens in Edinburgh, where it has been perfected.

This is the kind of bed which is planted with heathers that grow on peat or turf, a perfect material for plant roots. That is also the reason why peat is the main ingredient of modern potting compost.

There is very little nutritional value in it, but the structure of the material is fantastic, and in addition it can absorb and retain a great deal of moisture. However, you must take good care that the peat does not dry out.

A peat bed has no rocks or stones. It is nothing but acid soil that is mixed with peat up to a considerable depth: 2 parts peat to 2 parts soil with 1 part sand.

Sedum sempervivoides
*also flourishes in a
bird bath.*

That is why it may seem illogical to include a peat bed in a book about rock gardens. A peat bed certainly belongs here because you often come across valleys with damp, acid soil in the mountains. The plants which grow there are not rock plants but alpine plants. Rock garden enthusiasts use this peat bed to augment their collection with acid-loving plants. It is a supplement to the rock garden.

Another advantage of this type of peat bed is that it is simple and cheap to lay out.

You only need to change the conditions slightly by adding a little lime or scree to the peat to use it for an even greater selection of plants.

Sempervivum arach-
noides *is a suitable
plant for a bird bath or
on roof tiles.*

The bed can be slightly sloping, requires a lot of moisture, and must be well drained.

You can also manage this with a generous amount of scree or gravel. You can create some contours by using peat blocks to make walls. Plants flourish well on this ground and grow all over the wall, making it stronger.

Peat-loving plants usually grow in wooded areas which means that they like shade, so you can also site a peat bed in the problem areas on the shady side of your garden. In no time you have made something attractive in a difficult situation.

A peat bed is an especially good solution in our rainy climate. It is not worth thinking about in an area with little rain unless you include a sprinkler system.

As already mentioned, turf cannot be allowed to dry out, so it is better to dig the blocks into the ground.

Before you start building the peat bed, make sure the ground is totally free of weeds and that the materials with which you are working are sufficiently damp.

If you decide to build a wall around your peat bed, then it goes without saying that it should lean inwards slightly.

The construction of a peat bed is the same as for a raised bed, but in this case peat is the basis for the plants.

Onosma alborosea thrives in a sheltered spot in full sun, on walls or in a gravel bed.

43

Some of the poten-tillas are unsuitable for the rock garden because they grow too big but some are small enough to be included.

You must still pack the earth between the blocks, otherwise it will end up being far too loose.

The members of the *Ericaceae* family can be considered for the peat bed, including types of heath.

These, however, are not the most interesting plants for a peat bed. There are other very nice plants which belong to this family, including *Pernettya*, a delightful little shrub with white or purple berries which stay on the plant for most of the winter.

The smaller *Gaultheria* species and *Leucothoe* with its arching stems are shrubs suited to the peat bed. Add a few nice perennials and you will have a peat bed which is attractive throughout the year. Consider the relatively new *Corydalis flexuosa* with its pretty blue flowers, *Codonopsis*, *Epimedium*, *Lewisia*, *Primula*, and the many other acid-loving plants.

You can also create a type of rubble bed in a trough.

A gravel or scree bed

A lot of rock plants also flourish on gravel, or broken rocks, known as scree, even if there is limited space. Pile up a thick layer of small and large rocks. Mix some clay with garden soil and combine this with the rocks.

You can enjoy this bed during the whole year. But as with all of them, you can also make a beautiful and reasonable bed by placing it in a part of the garden which is as sunny as possible. The plants which flourish in gravel or scree beds like to have dry leaves and loose soil, such as *Onosma alborosea*, *Dianthus alpinus*, *Campanula cochle-ariifolia*, *Edraianthus graminifolius*, *Phlox subulata*, and *Morisia monanthus*.

Tufa Your favourite rock plants can also grow on tufa. You can use this rock in many different ways.

It is light and therefore easy to move, very porous, and can hold a good deal of water which can then be slowly taken up by the plants. Of course, during a prolonged period of dry weather it can also dry out completely, but to avoid this you can make a channel through the stones before you arrange them. This will provide enough moisture when it is very dry.

Try *Physoplexis comosum* or *Campanula zoysii* on tufa and you will be pleasantly surprised by the results. *Jankaea*, a difficult plant for the beginner, seems to do well on tufa.

Troughs and containers Growing plants in troughs or containers has the advantage of everything being easily accessible, as in raised beds. Plants which rot easily have a much better chance of survival in a container or trough, as long as you have provided for good drainage. In addition, it is a good method of gardening for people who have difficulty bending over. In a trough you can decide for yourself whether you want to work with acid- or lime-loving plants.

These wonderful troughs at Wisley might give you some ideas. Take special note of their shape.

Gardening in troughs is very fashionable at the moment. Nowadays there are lots of very beautiful troughs and containers on sale but unfortunately they are often expensive. After shopping around for some time you will eventually come across a reasonably priced trough or container. Even though there are many plants which are suitable for a trough or container, I shall only mention a few.

You can plant *Anchusa caespitosa*, *Potentilla nitida*, *Sedum*, *Sempervivum*, *Dianthus*, *Iris*, and *Acantholimon* in direct sunlight. You can plant *Ajuga*, *Saxifraga*, *Haberlea*, *Ramonda*, ferns, and *Cyclamen* corms in the shade. The dwarf shrubs such as *Salix reticulata*, *Daphne petraea* 'Grandiflora', and *Chamaecyparis obtusa* are also suitable.

Different kinds of trough

In the past troughs were made of sandstone. These days they are usually difficult to obtain and thus very expensive. Concrete troughs came along later and seemed to offer a reasonable alternative which was not too expensive. However, the combination of concrete and rock plants is not very attractive. Concrete containers or troughs have sharp forms and therefore people went in search of a material which was more attractive with rock plants. The solution arrived at was the so-called "hypertufa" mixture, a combination of sharp sand, peat, and cement which seemed to be the ideal solution for making troughs for rock plants. Troughs made from hypertufa are comparable with the

This home-made hypertufa container soon looks old because it quickly acquires a layer of moss.

old-fashioned troughs because the material has a nicer texture and weathers quickly. The use of peat in the ingredients for this mixture, encourages mosses and algae to establish themselves quickly, and that is what everyone likes to see: a weathered, natural-looking trough.

In the Alpine House at Wisley there are so many beautiful plants.

Making your own troughs

You can make your own troughs if you cannot find a reasonably priced example among the large selection that is available. Take a look at the spot in the garden or on the terrace where you will be placing the trough and decide what size it will be. Do not make the trough too chunky – the more elegant, the better. An oblong form still seems the best. If you want to assemble a large selection of plants then it is sensible not to make it too small. You will only need a few things – two cardboard boxes of unequal size (one must be 15cm (6in) wider, taller, and longer than the other) or wooden planks (for making the frame), a couple of laths or battens, lengths of drainpipe, a large sheet of plastic, and a piece of thick, plastic-coated gauze to prevent freezing. If you want to make a small trough which you bring indoors during the winter then just use two cardboard boxes. You do not need any plastic-covered gauze insulation because you will always bring the trough indoors during the winter. For a larger trough it is better to use a supporting frame for the mould. If you make a wooden frame, use separate lengths of wood which you can easily put together and pull apart. Carry out all the work on the large sheet of plastic.

T I P
Covering the bare ground between plants with coarse sand will discourage weeds from growing there.

Meconopsis horridula, *a gorgeous blue-flowered poppy, likes a cool, damp, slightly shaded spot.*

To make the construction with cardboard boxes, use the following method: Push the pipes for drainage through the lower walls of the outermost, larger box. Then use the laths to prop up the inner box until the top comes to the same height as the outer box.

Make a mixture of 2 parts cement, 2 parts peat, and 3 parts sand, adding enough water to make a thick porridge. Pour this cement into the outer box until it reaches the level of the laths and then reposition the small box on top of it. Fill the resulting cavity with mortar, pressing it down firmly with a wooden spatula the whole time.

Smooth the top neatly then allow the mortar to solidify for 1-2 days before carefully removing the moulds. After a few weeks you can position the troughs and fill them with soil and plants.

For a wooden construction the method is slightly more complicated because you have to position the layer of plastic-covered mesh in the bottom of the outermost case, so that it ends up permanently fixed in the dried cement. In addition, you must construct the casing with screws so that you can remove the frame easily. Otherwise the method is as described above.

Kitchen sinks

In England it is very common to use old, glazed earthenware instead of a trough. Since the discovery in the 1930s that rock plants could be grown very well in troughs and containers, people have exploited every possibility.

Jancaea heldreichii *is difficult to grow but does, however, do very well on tufa.*

Before they are planted these kitchen sink containers are coated with
a hypertufa mixture (1 part sand, 1 part peat dust, and 1 part damp
cement).

Smear a thick layer on the exterior of the container and let the mixture
dry out for a few weeks.

Turn the container over, cover the plug hole with broken pots and
fill it with a good soil mixture – for example, 1 part potting compost,
1 part rotted leaf mould or garden compost, and 1 part stone chippings. Leave this to stand for a few weeks before you plant anything.
You can also place a few stones between the plants.

Cover the soil with a thin layer of stone chippings or fine gravel.
Do not forget to water the plants regularly during the growing season,
enough for it to drip out of the plug hole.

Bird baths   In these cheap dishes, which can be bought in a shop which sells pet
supplies, you can start off by cultivating *Sedum* and *Sempervivum*.
It is not tricky and requires very little space.

Even before you consider the idea of starting a rock garden, you can
make something attractive out of these containers.

Roof tiles   You can even do lovely things with rock plants on your roof.
If you have a sloping roof with traditional tiles, you can put all sorts of
Sempervivum (houseleek) on it.

Primula auricula *is a
good choice for the
roof. In contrast to the
other* Primula *species
it can grow in dry,
poor soil.*

The idea is just the same as with bird dishes, but here the plants grow on your roof.

Once you have started with easily cultivated plants, you can experiment with other creepers and cushion-forming rock plants.

The rock garden in Prague also provides you with plenty of ideas for your own garden.

Eternite containers and dishes

Eternite containers were used much more often in the past than today.

They fell from favour because they used to contain asbestos. Now there are containers on sale which no longer contain asbestos and there is nothing to prevent you from making use of them. Eternite is an excellent, easily manoeuvred, lightweight material which is sold in all shapes and sizes.

Glazed stoneware pipes

People sometimes have to be creative and inventive. An old stoneware pipe is very handy, and offers a wonderful place to grow rock plants. Do not forget to drill drainage holes in it.

Cultivation in a cold frame, or greenhouse

If your hobby is already so far advanced that you want to collect the varieties which are difficult to cultivate in our climate, then a frame is perhaps the appropriate place to keep your treasured plants.

Particularly during the winter or if it suddenly turns very wet for a few days, you can provide safe accommodation for your plants. You can prevent them drying out by burying them deeply.

The alpine house   If you really want to do it seriously, then a special greenhouse for rock plants is a good investment. The rock plants are grown in pots and then sunk in trays which can be filled with potting compost. You can cultivate the plants here. The trays are usually expensive aluminium tables. Of course you could think up a cheaper alternative. If you have a greenhouse, then you have to ensure that there is good ventilation, because ventilation is essential for rock plants.

Plants which can be grown in the alpine house include *Dionysion*, *Androsace hirtella*, *Calceolaria darwinii*, *Raoulia eximea*, *Jancaea heldreichii*, and delicate violets.

Following pages:
The seed heads of
Dryas octopetala *are*
very striking.

Lewisia brachycalix *x*
rediviva *requires extra*
attention.

Codonopsis clematidea
is actually a climbing
plant, but it can also
fill in all sorts of
nooks and crannies.

Suitable plants

This chapter contains information about the features, cultivation, and propagation of a large number of plants which are suitable for your rock garden.

Acaena (Rosaceae) – pirri-pirri-bur
This is a genus of evergreen shrubs and annuals.
In very harsh winters, this semi-deciduous sub-shrub loses its leaves. It can be propagated by division or from seed.
Acaena buchananii is a hardy, low-growing, ground-cover plant suitable for poor soil, between paving stones, and around bulbs. This variety has bright green leaves and small orange-brown flowers. The cultivar 'Copper Carpet' has bronze-coloured leaves and greenish-red bracts.
A Microphylla has rust-coloured leaves and dark red flowers, while the cultivar 'Blue Haze' has grey leaves with brown flowers.

Acantholimon (Plumbaginaceae)
A genus of evergreen perennials that

are grown for their compact, cushion-forming, prickly leaves. They are very suitable for walls and in the rock garden.
They like a sunny position and are completely frost hardy, although they must be protected against heavy rain and very wet conditions. They can be raised from cuttings.
Acantholimon armemum has prickly leaves and striking seed heads.
A. venustum is an evergreen ground-cover plant that grows to no more than 15cm (6in) in height. The pink star-shaped flowers appear in May and June, growing on 3cm (1in) stems.
The blue-green leaves have a silvery fringe.
This variety is very suitable for an alpine house, preferring a very warm, well-drained position.

A. glumaceum is an evergreen, cushion-forming plant with hard, prickly, dark green leaves and pink star-shaped flowers in the summer. It grows to about 15cm (6in) in height with about twice the spread.

**Achillea (Compositae)
yarrow or milfoil**
This is a wonderful, trouble-free, hardy perennial.
Some varieties of this flower can be dried.
They enjoy sunny positions, and can be raised from cuttings in autumn or spring.
It actually benefits them to be divided regularly and replanted. Many species grow much too vigorously and too tall to be appropriate for the rock garden, but the following are suitable: *Achillea ageratifolia*, formerly *Anthemis aizoon*, with its

silver-grey, toothed leaves, and white flowers, grows to about 20cm (8in) high.

A.clavennae also has white flowers and deeply-cut silvery leaves.

It is half-hardy and dislikes damp winters, so it is better to plant it in a trough or raised bed.

Aethionema (Cruciferae)

This is a short-lived, usually ever-green shrub, sub-shrub, or perennial plant.

The plant seeds itself and can be propagated from stem cuttings.

Aethionema armemum is a sub-shrub that is sometimes evergreen while another year the blue-green leaves will be partially shed.

It is approximately 20cm (8in) high and blooms in the summer with pretty pink flowers.

It is better to cut these off straight after flowering, unless you want your garden to be filled with them. A 'Warley Ruber' has deep pink flowers.

A. grandiflorum (Persian stone cress) is somewhat taller than the rest, about 30cm (12in).

It has oval, blue-green leaves and heads of pale pink flowers in the summer.

Alchemilla alpina (Rosaceae) – lady's mantle

From the genus *Alchemilla* I will mention only the species with silvery-grey leaves, *A. alpina*.

It is about 15cm (6in) high and has a 25cm (10in) spread.

The most attractive feature of the lady's mantle is that dew or rain-drops remain on the leaves for a long time.

It is a hardy plant with greenish-

yellow flowers, ideal as a bedding plant. It can be propagated by divi-sion and also seeds itself.

Alyssum (Cruciferae)

This plant is completely hardy and grows on rocks and stony ground.

It can be propagated from half-ripe cuttings in late autumn or grown from seed in the spring.

Alyssum saxatile (syn. *Aurinia saxatilis*) is a hardy perennial with oval hairy grey-green leaves which blooms profusely in late spring and early summer with bright yellow flowers.

Some of the cultivars that are worth considering include 'Gold Dust' with its bright yellow flowers, and 'Variegatum' with yellow flowers and creamy-white edged leaves.

A. montanum, is a 25cm (10in) high, evergreen plant which grows

Aquilegia flabellata *'Ministar' is a must for the rock garden.*
Left: Androsace sempervivoides *is easy to grow.*
Previous pages:
Edraianthus serypyllifolius *has deep violet flowers on short stems.*

along the ground or upright, with green to white rosettes of foliage and bright yellow flowers.
In the mountains this plant grows on sandy, rocky, or stony ground. The cultivar *A. m.* 'Mountain Gold' has yellow flowers from April to June. It is about 15cm (6in) high.

Anacyclus (Compositae)

With this group of plants, the stems grow from a central rhizome. Anacyclus can be propagated from seed in autumn or from cuttings in spring.
The plants are perennial and prefer a sunny position on well-drained ground.
Anacyclus depressus is a short-lived hardy plant.
It has pretty white flowers which close if the weather is overcast.

It does not like wet winters and will not survive a harsh winter.

Anchusa angustissima caespitosa (Boraginaceae)

An evergreen, hardy plant with arrow-shaped, dark green foliage which is not easy to cultivate.
The bright blue flowers, with a white heart, appear in spring among the leaf rosettes.
The plant is about 5cm (2in) high and spreads to about 20cm (8in). Old plants flower less well.
Propagate from cuttings in early summer. It is very suitable for a raised bed, a gravel bed, or an alpine house.

Androsace (Primulaceae)

A genus of cushion-forming evergreens or annuals, sometimes with hairy leaves.

They can be propagated from stem cuttings or seed.
Mildew and aphids can be a problem.
Androsace carnea is a more difficult species, with evergreen, hairy leaves and a few small pink flowers that grow on stems rising above the leaf rosettes during spring.
It grows to about 5cm (2in) and is suitable for a trough.
A. c. ssp. *laggeri* is a 5cm (2in) high evergreen, cushion-forming hardy plant with deep pink flowers above the cushions.
These plants also do well in a trough or raised bed.
A. lanuginosa is at most a 4cm (1 1/2in) high, evergreen plant with silky, hairy, silver-grey foliage.
It is a mat-forming plant that spreads to about 18cm (7in) across.

It produces lovely pink to lavender-blue flowers with a dark centre from summer through to autumn and needs a sunny and well-drained position. It is very hardy.

The variety *A. leichtlinii* has pale pink flowers.

A. primuloides is an evergreen, mat-forming hardy plant which only grows about 5cm (2in) high.

The flat, bright pink flowers have yellow centres.

It is a very hardy plant with rosettes of silvery, hairy leaves.

It is an ideal rock plant which prefers a reasonably humid habitat.

The ground-hugging *A. vandelii* (syn. *A. imbricata*) is only about 2.5cm (1in) high, an evergreen hardy plant with small stemless, white flowers above its rosettes of hairy leaves.

The flowers appear in spring and have yellow hearts that turn red. This plant likes neutral soil.

Antennaria (Compositae) – cat's ears

This is a genus with beautiful flowers that grow on stems with hairy leaves. The plants form an excellent carpet.

They can be propagated by division in spring or from seed.

They grow on any kind of soil.

Antennaria dioica is a semi-evergreen, ground-cover plant which does not grow more than 5cm (2in) high.

This plant is a delight with small, woolly, oval, grey-white leaves, and white or pale pink flowers which appear in early summer.

There are two cultivars, the deep pink 'Nywoods' and the rose-red 'Rosea'.

Gypsophila aretioides is a good plant for tufa and rubble.

Aquilegia (Ranunculaceae) – columbine

This is a genus of remarkable but short-lived perennials for the whole garden.

They are not usually difficult to grow. They seed themselves freely, with the result that they do not always reproduce the same form.

Aquilegia flabellata is a wonderful hardy plant for the rock garden; it is about 20cm (8in) high and has blue and creamy-white flowers.

A.f. 'Mini Star' is smaller than the rest of this family and has lilac and creamy-white flowers.

Aquilegia flabellata var. *pumila* with creamy-white and lilac-blue flowers grows to a height of about 15cm (6in). At 30cm (12in),

Cypripedium calceolus *var.* pubescens.

Left: A close-up of Codonopsis clematidae *shows its sheer beauty.*

Opposite page: Asperula sintenisii *'Puberula' flowers in April and May.*

A. *viridiflora* is slightly taller than A. *flabellata*, and has brownish-red flowers with green sepals.

Arenaria (Caryophyllaceae) – sandwort

This genus of spring- and summer-flowering annuals and perennials likes a sunny position and sandy soil. The plants can be grown from seed or stem cuttings.
Arenaria balearica, with its delicate, compact, evergreen carpet of small hairy leaves, grows best on tufa or other type of porous, stony surface.
It is only 2cm (1in) high.
In very harsh winters it can freeze. The white flowers appear in late spring.
It originates in the mountains on islands in the Mediterranean. A. *montana* is a grey-green, fine-

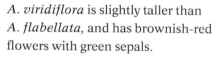

haired, carpeting plant with erect stalks about 5cm (2in) tall on which the white flowers grow.
It thrives on a garden wall or a slope. A. *purpurascens* is an ever--green, mat-forming plant with shiny, pointed leaves, and pale to deep pink flowers in early spring. The plant is about 2cm (1in) tall.
A. *tetraquetra* has white, star-shaped flowers in May and is very suitable for a container or the alpine greenhouse.
This plant is also evergreen, and its small leaves form a grey-green cushion. It is about 5cm (2in) high.

Armeria (Plumbaginaceae) – sea pink

There are various species of sea pink. They can be cultivated from softwood stem cuttings or from seed. The plant thrives in a sunny

position on coarse, well-drained soil.
Among the species suitable for the rock garden are *Armeria juniperifolia*, an evergreen, hardy, cushion-forming plant with soft pink flowers in late spring and early summer.
A. *maritima* is a completely hardy plant, whose vivid pink flowers stand out above its tussock of grass-like leaves. There is also a white cultivar, A. *m.* 'Alba'.

Artemisia (Compositae) – wormwood

There are also many different species in this genus, including hardy perennials and sub-shrubs of which some are evergreen.
They are almost always planted for their beautiful foliage.
Not all artemisias are completely hardy.

The dwarf species in particular find wet and severe winters a problem. They respond to being cut back a little in the spring. *Artemisia pedemontana* is a low, compact, hardy plant with upright stems.
It blooms from July to September with insignificant yellow flowers so it is primarily grown for its grey foliage.
In mountainous regions it grows on rocks, scree slopes, and moraine.
A. schmidtiana 'Nana' is a semi-evergreen perennial with feathery, silvery foliage, but it is not completely hardy. It blooms in summer with unremarkable, yellow flowers and is very suitable for walls.

Asarina (Scrophulariaceae)

This genus includes evergreen climbing plants and standard evergreen perennials.

They are not completely hardy and must be protected if the temperature falls below 5 °C.
They like very well-drained soil and a sunny position.
Asarina procumbens is very suitable for walls or the rock garden.
It is a low, trailing plant, with wonderful, pale yellow flowers and semi-evergreen, soft, hairy leaves. This plant occasionally freezes, but in the right place it will seed itself.

Asarum (Aristolochiaceae) – asarabacca

This is a genus of perennials, some of which are evergreen.
They usually have heart- or kidney-shaped leaves and make good ground cover. In a harsh winter the leaves may suffer even though the plant is hardy.

They prefer a shady spot in damp, humus-rich soil.
They can be propagated by division and seed themselves.
Asarum europaeum is a sturdy, evergreen perennial with shiny, green, kidney-shaped leaves under which the small, brown flowers appear in spring.
The plant is about 15cm (6in) high.

Asperula (Rubiaceae)

This genus includes perennials and annuals, some of which are very suitable for the alpine house.
Most varieties are hardy, while the annuals seed themselves freely.
Normally they like a sunny position, well-drained soil, and water in the summer.
Asperula suberosa is a perennial which produces a profusion of pale pink flowers.

Campanula waldsteiniana *only grows to 12-15cm (5-6in) and is native to the former Yugoslavia.*

Right:
Campanula zoysii, *with its pastel blue flowers, is quite a difficult plant to grow.*

Opposite page:
The distinctive flowers of Primula vialii *are very striking.*

It is a tussock-forming plant suitable for the alpine house or a trough.
It is rather fussy about humidity – it does not like wet winters yet requires a damp spot during the summer.
It grows about 10cm (3in) high and spreads to 30cm (12in).

Aster (Compositae) – Michaelmas daisy

The family of the *Compositae* includes a great many species, including the Michaelmas daisies.
Most of these are perennials but there are also evergreen and deciduous sub-shrubs.
They can survive in vitually any soil although a slightly fertile soil is very valuable.
Some varieties have trouble with mildew, usually the new forms of *Aster novibelgii* which are suitable for the rock garden.

They can also suffer from various insect pests.
You can propagate them easily by division or shoot cuttings.
A. alpinus is suitable for the rock garden, as well as a selection of cultivars which are for sale at nurseries.
It is a small perennial which blooms from July to September, with violet, yellow-centred flowers.
It is a native of rocky areas and mountain meadows in central and south-eastern Europe.
It grows about 15cm (6in) tall and is hardy. The cultivar 'Goliath' has white flowers.

Aubrieta (Cruciferae)

A genus of evergreen, cushion-forming, trailing plants suitable for walls and rock gardens.
They grow naturally in rocky places.

They like a sunny position and are hardy.
To keep them in shape, trim back after flowering.
They are propagated by stem cuttings and division.
Aubrieta deltoidea has deep pink flowers.
There are many cultivars in a number of colours including white, blue, purple, and pink.
A.d. 'Argenteo variegata' has green leaves splashed with creamy white, and produces pinkish-lavender flowers.

Campanula (Campanulaceae) – bellflower

In general these are herbaceous plants which grow and flower easily in a well-drained soil.
Many of the species can be grown in the rock garden.

They flower in full sun, and half-shaded situations, with pretty, bell-shaped flowers.

A very large number are suitable for the rock garden.

They can easily be grown from seed, but they can also be propagated from stem or root cuttings.

Campanula alpestris (syn. *C. allionii*) grows 10-15cm (4-6in) high with arrow-shaped leaves and bell-shaped flowers.

It has a root-stock under the ground. The plant likes lime-free soil. Its blue-purple flowers appear in early summer.

It is also suitable for a frame.

C. arvatica is about 10cm (4in) tall and in the middle of summer produces violet-blue flowers.

It is suitable for the alpine house.

There is also a very good, white, hardy cultivar 'Alba'.

C. aucheri forms a 5cm (2in) high mat and has thick roots and large, deep purple flowers that can be 2.5cm (1in) long.

It flowers in summer and is hardy.

C. 'Birch Farm Hybrid' is a strong, evergreen perennial.

It has pretty, bell-shaped, deep violet flowers in the summer.

C. betulifolia has trailing, delicate, stems.

In summer the plants have white to pink flowers which are dark pink on the inside.

The leaves are wedge-shaped and the plant is hardy.

C. carpatica is a species with a great many cultivars whose flowers vary from white to dark blue in colour.

It grows about 10cm (4in) tall and spreads 30cm (12in) across.

It has bell-shaped flowers in summer and is hardy.

C. cochleariifolia forms a root-stock and has small, round leaves. It has a spreading growth form. White, lavender, or light blue flowers appear in clusters during the summer, and the plant is about 10cm (4in) tall.

In the mountains it grows on rocks, scree slopes, and alpine meadows, and is hardy.

C. excisa also forms a root-stock and has small leaves.

The nodding, lilac-blue flowers appear in early summer.

It likes acid soil and is an easy plant to cultivate for the rock-garden.

Celmisia (Compositae)

One of the group of New Zealand's native evergreen perennials, which is not hardy in western Europe.

A collection of Lewisia *species in full bloom is a lovely sight.*

Right: The well-known Primula auricula.

Opposite page: Various species of Hieracium *grow in the alpine meadows, mainly on dry ground.*

Here it is only suitable for the alpine house.
Most varieties have daisy-like flowers in late spring and the early summer.
They usually have lovely leaves.
They like acid, well-drained, sandy soil.
They can be propagated from seed or cuttings in the early spring.
There are a number of varieties available in Great Britain at specialist nurseries.
There is a good display in the alpine house at Wisley.
Celmisia bellidioides is at most 2cm (3/4in) tall and is a carpeting perennial with dark green, leathery, round leaves, and white flowers.
Celmisia coriacea has sword-shaped, silvery leaves, and bears white flowers in the summer.
At 30cm (12in) it is rather taller.

Cerastium (Carophyllaceae) – mouse-ear

In this genus there are two species which are suitable for the rock garden.
They are easily cultivated perennials or occasionally annuals, which make very satisfactory ground cover.
Cerastium alpinum grows on rocks and scree slopes in the Alps and the polar regions.
It is about 10cm (4in) high and has silver-grey foliage which is covered with masses of white, star-shaped flowers. *C. tomentosum* is known as "snow in the summer" because it also has masses of little white flowers which hide the foliage.
It also has silver-grey leaves which are hairy. It is a very rewarding plant which flourishes in a warm, sunny spot.

Chrysanthemum (Compositae)

Although this is a very large genus with very few requirements regarding soil-type, there are not many which are useful in the rock garden, apart from *Chrysanthemum cinerariifolia* which is also sold as *Tanacetum cinerariifolium*.
The plants form beautiful clumps with daisy-like flowers.
The classification of the chrysanthemums usually causes a lot of problems: *Matricaria*, *Tanacetum*, *Achillea*, and *Chrysanthemum* are all interchanged with each other.
I have kept to *Chrysanthemum* because I find this the simplest.
Most types of chrysanthemum are too large for the rock garden, but *C. argenteum* (syn. *Tanacetum argenteum*) is a species that could be suitable, with silver-grey, bushy foliage.

There is also *C. haradjanii* (*Tanacetum haradjanii*) with its evergreen, mat-forming, silver-grey foliage, and bright yellow flowers. It is suitable for the rock garden and the alpine house. It grows to about 25cm (10in).

Codonopsis (Campanulaceae)

From this genus I will only mention *Codonopsis clematidae*, a climbing plant which can also be used as a trailing plant, and therefore can find a home in the rock garden. It can be grown from seed.

Convolvulus sabatius (Convolvulaceae)

A pretty, creeping plant for the alpine house which is not hardy. The azure-blue flowers appear in summer through into early autumn. The plant has pretty, grey-green leaves and likes a sunny position on well-drained soil. It is propagated from shoot cuttings.

Cotula (Compositae)

There are aquatic as well as terrestrial plants in this genus.
Most of them are evergreen plants with lovely little leaves and button-like flower heads.
They vary from almost to completely hardy and prefer a sunny, not too dry position.
They can be divided easily.
Cotula atrata (syn. *Leptinella atrata*) is a hardy, evergreen, mat-forming plant with finely divided leaves, and flower heads which appear in spring that are almost black.
The plant is about 2.5cm (1in) high and forms a cushion easily.
It is a difficult plant to grow. It is best cultivated in an alpine house. One of the first plants which I came across at school was *Cotula squalida* (*Leptinella squalida*).
This species also has finely divided foliage but, in contrast to the previous species, it is relatively easy to cultivate and flourishes on any type of soil.
It spreads rapidly but is also easy to weed out. It is primarily a lovely, ground-cover plant to surround other plants that do not like their roots being disturbed. It is only 2.5cm (1in) high.

Crepis (Compositae) – hawk's beard

These are summer-blooming annuals, biennials or perennials, some of which are evergreen.
The leaves grow in flat rosettes.
There are varieties which could be

Cypripedium calceolus *is a terrestrial*
orchid.

Right:
Aubrieta *'Eileen Longstar' has to be*
trimmed back after flowering.

Opposite page:
The big, beautiful flowers of Lewisia
tweedyi *bloom in an alpine house*
during April.

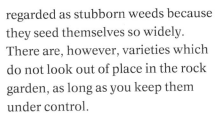

regarded as stubborn weeds because
they seed themselves so widely.
There are, however, varieties which
do not look out of place in the rock
garden, as long as you keep them
under control.
Crepis aurea grows about 20cm
(8in) high with light green leaves
and has orange, dandelion-like
flowers in summer. The stems are
covered in black and white hairs. It
is native to mountain meadows.

Cypripedium (Cypripediaceae) – slipper orchid

This is a genus of herbaceous perennials with a rhizome or creeping
root-stock.
They are so-called terrestrial
orchids. The plants are grown for
their extraordinary flowers.
Cypripedium calceolus (the lady's
slipper orchid), is a yellow-flowered

orchid which has a dark-veined lip
with red spots. It grows in the
mountain forests and even though it
is not strictly a rock plant I want to
mention it here.
You will not find it in the catalogues
of rock-garden nurseries, but at the
orchid nurseries instead. Raising it
from seed is a specialist procedure.
C. pubescens, from North America,
is also a yellow-flowered species but
its leaves are larger and hairy.

Dactylorhiza (Orchidaceae) – marsh orchid

This plant belongs to the orchid
family and is easily recognizable as
such. Some species in this genus
were previously classified under
Orchis.
Orchids are often epiphytic, that is
they grow on other plants without
taking nutrients from the host.

This genus is, however, terrestrial.
Dactylorhiza majalis (the broad-
leaved marsh orchid), has quite
large, pale to deep purple flowers.
Do not use any artificial manure on
the *Dactylorhiza* species because it
is fatal.
That has already happened too
often in the wild.
They are still found in damp, non-
improved pastures, marshes, and
alpine meadows.
D. maculata (the heath spotted
orchid), has spotted leaves and pale
lilac, white or mauve flowers on
fragile stalks.
These plants do well in a peat bed
because they like an acid soil.
In the wild you can still find them in
acid pastures, heathlands, and
upland moors.
All orchid species in the wild are
fully protected by law.

Aster alpinius *'Albus' is a very rewarding plant for the rockery.*

Left:
Dianthus haematocalyx *ssp.* pindicola.

Opposite page:
Although the startling pale blue flowers make it such a wonderful plant, Meconopsis betonicifolia *is unfortunately too tall for the rock garden.*

Dianthus (Caryophyllaceae) – pink
This is a very large genus of perennials and biennials. They bloom in summer and often have sweet-scented flowers. Many are too big for the rock garden, but there are plenty of others which grow an flower magnificently in a fair-sized rock garden, in troughs, containers, or on walls. They can be propagated from seed and in some cases from cuttings.
Sometimes they have problems with rust, and a virus which is spread by aphids.
Dianthus alpinus (alpine pink), is an evergreen, low-growing pink which has pink flowers from May through to the middle of summer. It likes a rich soil and grows about 10cm (4in) high.
D. deltoides is sometimes called the maiden pink. It grows to about

15cm (6in) and has white, pink, or cherry-red flowers. It forms a loose mass of leaves which are sometimes blue-green. It is advisable to trim it back after flowering.
D.d. 'Flashing Light' has lovely, cerise flowers.
D. gratianopolitanus (syn. D. *caesius*), the Cheddar pink, and its many cultivars are about 15cm (6in) tall and produce flat, pale pink, scented flowers in early summer. It has small, grey-green leaves.
D. haematocalyx is suitable for a gravel bed or scree. It grows about 15cm (6in) tall and has dark pink flowers in June.
D. microlepis is only about 5cm (2in) high and has light pink flowers in the early summer. This is most suitable for a trough.
D. myrtinervis is an evergreen, low-growing perennial with pink flowers

above grass-like foliage. This is only a small selection from the many pinks which are suitable for the rock garden.

Dodecatheon (Primulaceae) – shooting star
I find this plant a problem because it disappears so soon after flowering. Always make a note of where you have planted it. The flowers appear in spring and summer. As soon as the flowers are pollinated they turn to face the sky. They like a damp habitat so they find the lower part of the rock garden preferable. Some sun or semi-shade is good for them. *Dodecatheon dentatum* is about 10cm (4in) high and has lovely white flowers in late spring. It likes a shady position. *D. meadia* is a 20cm (8in) tall perennial with light green leaves and pale pink flowers.

It also likes to be situated in half-shade. *D.m.* 'Album' is the white cultivar.

D. pulchellum is about 15cm (6in) high with dark cerise flowers.

Douglasia (Primulaceae)

These are evergreen perennials which flower abundantly in spring and can be propagated by cuttings or from seed. They are not very easy plants, preferring an alpine house or scree slope. They like a sunny but not too dry position. *Douglassia laevigata* (syn. *Androsace laevigata*) produces pink flowers in the spring. It displays its fringed flowers high above the leaves and is only about 10cm (4in) in height.

Draba (Cruciferae)

This is a genus of mostly cushion- or mat-forming perennials which grow on rocks in mountainous regions. They like full sun and gritty, well-drained soil. In addition, some of them cannot survive wet winters. Propagate *Draba* by taking the shoots from the leaf rosettes, or grow from seed. *Draba aizoides* is a semi-evergreen, mat-forming plant which grows about 5cm (2in) high and has vivid yellow flowers in spring. *D. mollisima* forms a small cushion of green foliage covered with small yellow flowers in spring so that the plant looks like a yellow globe. *D. polytricha* is a plant which very much likes the alpine house, where it produces golden-yellow flowers as early as March. *D. bryoides* var. *imbricata* also blooms with small yellow flowers in an alpine house. You can also plant it in a trough or on tufa.

Take special care because it is not hardy. If the winter is wet you must give it some protection.

Dryas octopetala (Rosaceae) – mountain avens

This a very hardy, ground-covering sub-shrub which is only 10cm (4in) high but can spread to about 60cm (2ft) across.

It has dark green, leathery leaves which resemble oak leaves. It is common on scree and steep rocky slopes. The white flowers appear in early summer. It is very suitable for growing beside water, on walls, and in the rock garden and likes full sun and gritty, well-drained, peaty soil. You can propagate it by division or from seed.

Edraianthus (Campanulaceae)

This is a summer-flowering genus which likes humus-rich soil in a

sunny position. The species resemble campanulas, and are propagated from stem cuttings. Some seed themselves.

Edraianthus graminifolius has purple-blue flowers and grows about 10cm (4in) tall.

E. pumilio is a short-lived variety with grass-like foliage. Its lavender-blue flowers appear on short stalks in the early summer. It is about 5cm (2in) tall.

E. serpyllifolius is a dwarf plant, only 1cm (1/3in) high. It has violet-blue flowers. The plant rarely seeds spontaneously.

Erigeron (Compositae) – fleabane

These plants are usually cultivated for their small, daisy-like flowers. They like a rather friable, porous, sandy soil in a sunny position. They are fussy about humidity.

Wet winters can be fatal but on the other hand they tend to dry out if they do not have sufficient water in the growing season.

Erigeron aurantiacus is a completely hardy plant with grey-green leaves and pretty golden orange flowers in the summer.

It can be propagated from seed or by cuttings.

E. aureus is a perennial which grows about 5cm (2in) high and 10cm (4in) across.

It is hardy and has spoon-shaped, hairy leaves.

It does not like very much rain in the winter, but it does like a blanket of snow. It is attacked by aphids.

E. karvinskianus is a perennial which is only about 10cm (4in) tall but tends to spread.

Unfortunately it is not very hardy but if you place a few tussocks in a

Primula marginata *flowers freely in spring. Its leaves look as if they are dusted with flour. It thrives in a sunny spot.*
Opposite page: Lithodora diffusa 'Heavenly Blue' with gentian blue flowers.

cool place during the winter, the next year you will have lovely plants again.

The small, daisy-like flowers vary in colour from white to pink. In a frost-free place it can seed itself.

Erodium (Geraniaceae) – stork's bill

This is a cushion-forming perennial which likes sun. It can be propagated from seed, by shoot cuttings, or sometimes by root cuttings.

Erodium chrysanthaarum blooms from the end of May through to the end of July with sulphur-coloured to

The needle-like foliage of the free-flowering Phlox subulata *'Scarlet Flame' makes it indispensible in the rock garden.*

Left:
Pulsatilla vernalis *prefers a dry position.*

Opposite page:
Pleione *'Hekla' is a distant cousin of the primulas and likes to be planted close to water.*

butter-yellow flowers emerging out of a tight cushion of silver-grey, fern-like leaves. It is about 25cm (10in) tall.

E. foetidum (syn. *E. petraeum*) is a compact perennial with oval, grey leaves above which the few red-veined flowers peek their heads in the summer.

E. cheianthifolium (syn. *E. p.* ssp. *crispum*) blooms in July and August with white, purple-spotted flowers. The plants are about 25cm (10in) tall. *E. rupestre* 'Stephanii' is a 10cm (4in) tall perennial which blooms for a long time with white, purple-spotted flowers.

Erysimum (Crucificae)

A genus which very much resembles *Cheiranthus* (wallflower), and of which at least one variety is not at all out of place in the rock garden.

Propagate members of this family by taking cuttings or from seed. *Erysimum helveticum* forms a tussock which is only 10cm (4in) high, and has fragrant flowers in late spring. It is semi-evergreen.

Euphorbia (Euphorbiaceae) – spurge

There are shrubs, succulents, annuals, and perennials in this genus. Some are evergreen, others semi-evergreen. Usually they like a moist, but well-drained soil and sun or half-shade. They can be propagated from cuttings, by division or from seed. Only *Euphorbia myrsinites* is suitable for the rock garden because the other species are too tall.

This one trails over the rock garden, so it does well on a wall or amongst the rocks.

Growing about 10cm (4in) tall, it

has evergreen, blue-grey foliage, and yellow-green flowers in the spring. It can freeze in very hard winters.

Euryops (Compositae)

This is a genus of evergreen and semi-evergreen sub-shrubs from South Africa.

They are not totally hardy in our climate and so need a sheltered situation.

Euryops acraeus has beautiful, narrow, grey leaves, and yellow flowers in June.

Fibigia clypeata (Crucificae)

This genus consists of upright, compact biennials or perennials with felt-like, grey foliage.

Fibigia clypeata can grow 45cm (18in) high and produces little, yellow flowers from April to June. It has striking, attractive seed cases

and can be grown from seed. It is a good plant for rocks and walls.

Gentiana (Gentianaceae) – gentian

This is a varied genus which includes annuals and biennials, as well as perennials, some of which are evergreen and some semi-evergreen. They have wonderful blue flowers and are perfectly suited to the rock garden, a trough, container or dish, as well as the peat bed.

They like sun or semi-shade and a humus-rich, rather damp soil varying from neutral to acid. Some species grow naturally on limestone soils in the wild. They can be propagated by division, from cuttings, or from seed in the autumn. A number of autumn-flowering varieties like to be divided and replanted in fresh soil.

Gentiana acaulis is an evergreen perennial with small, shiny leaves. In spring, as well as sometimes in the autumn, it has stunning, prominent blue flowers. The leaves are only 5cm (2in) long.

G. angustifolia is also an evergreen perennial which is a little taller than the previous species, approximately 10cm (4in). In the summer it is a definite asset in the garden, with its sky-blue flowers standing out above the rather insignificant leaves. It can tolerate acid soil. *G. asclepiadeae* (willow gentian) is actually too tall for the rock garden, but it is so beautiful that I cannot ignore it. It can grow up to 70cm (28in) tall and from the summer through to autumn it has dark blue flowers with stripes on the inside which stand out from the foliage. It does not like being transplanted, so just

enjoy it and leave well alone.

G. clusii is a plant which likes to be split every 3 or 4 years. It has azure-blue flowers in the summer. It can tolerate acid soil and is found in the Alps, the Apennines, and the Carpathian mountains.

G. lutea has the common name great yellow gentian, as you will have guessed from the word "lutea". It can grow up to 1m (3ft) high and blooms in the summer. *Gentiana x macaulayi* 'Well's Variety' is an evergreen, low-growing perennial that likes damp, acid soil. Its mid-blue flowers appear in the summer above its small leaves. Its natural habitat in the mountains is in the meadows and damp parts of the forest. *G. saxosa* is a white-flowered, evergreen perennial with dark green foliage. It is only short-lived and is suited to scree slopes.

G septemfida likes humus-rich soil but can also tolerate porous clay. Its mid-blue flowers appear in late summer. This perennial is evergreen and grows to about 20cm (8in).

G. sino-odorata is also an ever-green which has masses of single white flowers in the autumn. It likes damp, acid conditions.

Geranium (Geraniaceae) – cranesbill

This is a large genus of richly flower-ing perennials.

Cranesbills are propagated by seed or by cuttings, while the cultivars can be propagated by cuttings or division.

Geranium cinerium, which grows about 15cm (6in) high, is a semi-evergreen plant which forms cushions of grey-green leaves. It has deep pink flowers with a dark centre and dark stripes. The flowers appear from late spring onwards and continue into the autumn. 'Laurence Flatman' is a cultivar with pinkish-white striped flowers which is totally hardy and likes a sunny position with well-drained soil.

G. cinereum var. *subcaulescens* is about 10cm (4in) tall and has beautiful dark pink flowers with a black centre. The leaves are round and grey-green. It is completely hardy and likes well-drained soil and sun.

G. wallichianum had pretty lilac-pink flowers at Wisley from the end of July until September.

The cultivar 'Buxton's Blue' (syn. *G. w.* 'Buxton's Variety') has beautiful blue flowers with a white centre. They are plants which grow to a height of about 40cm (16in) and like half-shade. A single plant can easily grow up to 1m (3ft) across. They are not really difficult plants, and they are very useful because they start to flower so late.

Geum (Rosaceae) – avens

A genus of summer-flowering perennials for a sunny, well-drained position.

Geum montanum (alpine avens) is a perennial with a root-stock that only puts out a few runners. It blooms in the summer with golden-yellow flowers which are followed by brownish-yellow seed cases. It is very suitable for the rock garden and likes a sunny, moist, well-drained position. This plant can be propagated by division, cuttings, or seed. In the mountains it is found in rocky places and meadows.

G. reptans (creeping avens) is a

difficult plant which is only suited
to a damp gravel bed. Moreover, it is
a lime-hater and benefits more from
quite peaty ground.
It produces red creeping stems and
has bright yellow flowers. It can be
propagated by layering.

Globularia (Globulariaceae)

A genus of low shrubs or perennials,
the former being propagated by
cuttings, and the latter from seed.
In the rock garden *Globularia
cordifolia*, which has lavender-blue
flowers, is very attractive.
This plant forms an evergreen carpet
and is only 5cm (2in) high. It is
summer-flowering. In the wild it is
found on rocks and scree slopes.

Gypsophila (Caryophyllaceae)

These plants flower from spring
through to autumn.

They are annuals or perennials,
some of which are semi-evergreen.
They are all hardy, they like sun and
well-drained ground, but flourish
just as well on sandy, stony ground.
Propagate them in the summer from
cuttings or in the autumn from seed.
G. cerastioides is a ground-covering plant which grows from 10-
15cm (4-6in).
In the spring it has off-white, drooping flowers that open out from
lavender-coloured buds.
It is a rather difficult plant which is
also attacked by insect pests.
G. repens is a semi-evergreen
perennial with white, pink or lilac
flowers during the summer.
It is at most 5cm (2in) high and has
small, blue-green leaves.
'Dorothy Teacher' is a cultivar
with little white flowers which turn
pink.

Geranium sanguineum, *the bloody cranes-
bill, is a very robust plant.*

Opposite page: Draba bryoides *var.* imbricata, *sometimes called* D. rigida bryoides
'Imbricata' *has golden yellow flowers.*

Haberlea (Gesneriaceae)

These evergreen perennials form
rosettes. They grow well on walls
and like shade.
They can be propagated from seed,
leaf cuttings or offsets.
Haberlea rhodopensis grows to
about 10cm (4in) high and has hairy
leaves and violet flowers in May to
June. *H.r.* 'Virginalis' produces
white flowers in May.

Haplopappus coronopifolius
(Compositae)

This species, which is also called *H.
glutinosus*, is the only member of

Euryops acraeus *must have a sheltered position because it is not completely hardy.*

Left:
Gentiana saxosa *is a short-lived scree plant that is suitable for a trough.*

Opposite page:
Hepatica nobilis *is a rather poisonous plant, that was once used in remedies for coughs and chest complaints.*

this family that I want to mention here. It is a not very well-known sub-shrub with golden yellow daisy-like flowers, but it is not very hardy. It is very nice in a trough or container. Its leaves are dark green and leathery. It likes well-drained soil and a little sun.

Helichrysum (Compositae)

The genus *Helichrysum* includes the well-known everlasting flower. Enthusiasts know that there are many other beautiful species. Some of the plants are very suitable for the rock garden but they are not all hardy.
They will do well if you put them in a cool place, and protect them in winter. Generally they prefer gritty, well-drained soil and they dislike wet winters.
Helichrysum coralloides is an ever-

green plant with dark green, scaly leaves with remarkable silver-coloured markings. It occasionally produces yellow flowers. It hates a wet winter and is only suitable for the alpine house.
H. milfordiae is an evergreen, mat-forming sub-shrub which is often sold under its synonym *H. marginatum*.
It does not like damp winters and flourishes in an alpine house. On sunny days large, red buds appear which turn into white, daisy-like flowers. The leaf rosettes consist of silvery, hairy leaves. The plant is easily propagated in the spring by removing rosettes and replanting them.

Hepatica (Ranunculaceae)

This is a perennial which flowers in early spring. It is native to the

forested regions in central Europe. That is why it likes semi-shade and humus-rich ground. It can be grown from fresh seeds or propagated by division or stem cuttings in the autumn. The best known species is *Hepatica nobilis* (syn. *Anemone hepatica*), a fairly slow-growing, semi-evergreen plant.
It grows to no more than 10cm (4in) tall and its mid-green leaves and range of colours– white, pink, carmine red, and violet– make it very suitable for the rock garden.
H. transylvanica does not grow much taller and has flowers which are just as varied in colour. There are also double-flowered cultivars.

Hieracium amplexicaule (Compositae) – hawkweed

This is a 40cm (16in) high plant which is found in alpine meadows.

Hieracium is a very hardy plant which is particularly suitable for dry ground.

It has silver-grey leaves and flowers in the middle of summer. It seeds itself freely.

Hutchinsia alpina (Cruciferae)

This is a lovely plant for the rock garden, reaching about 10cm (4in), and it is not difficult to cultivate. Small white flowers decorate the dark green, fern-like leaves during the summer. It is often sold under its synonym *Thlaspi alpina*.

Iberis sempervirens (Cruciferae)

This is an evergreen, bushy perennial which grows up to 25cm (10in) and produces flattened, white flower heads in late spring and early summer.

Pruning it back hard after flowering is advisable. In the mountains it grows mainly on rocks, in crevices, and among stones.

It is easy to cultivate on poor soil. It can be propagated from semi-ripe cuttings in the summer. The plants are totally winter-hardy and like sun and well-drained ground.

Two beautiful cultivars are 'Little Gem' and 'Snowflake'.

Jancaea (Gesneriaceae)

Jancaea, sometimes written as *Jankaea*, is a plant for the alpine house.

It is mainly grown for its flowers and silver-green foliage. It is propagated from seed or leaf cuttings.

It is difficult to cultivate because it is quite fussy about soil type and humidity.

Jancaea heldreichii has splendid violet-coloured flowers in May which stand out above the rosettes of silver-green, hairy foliage.

Leontopodium alpinum (Compositae) – edelweiss

A short-lived perennial with a clump of arrow-shaped, woolly leaves. It has bunches of small, silver-white flowers which are surrounded by thick, felted, star-shaped bracts. It dislikes summer and winter wet. It grows about 15cm (6in) high and 4in (10cm) across, and flowers in June and July. It looks quite floppy, so *L.a.* ssp. *nivale* and *L.a.* 'Mignon' are more suitable. These two bloom later, between July and August.

They all like a dry, sunny position, and are totally hardy.

They can be grown from seed. In the wild they grow in alpine meadows, on scree slopes, and on rocks.

Native to the Balkans, Edraianthus pumilio *is a beautiful plant with bell-shaped flowers.*

Right:
Dianthus haemathocalyx *is a Greek plant with deep pink flowers.*

Opposite page: Raoulia australis *is a surface-rooting plant for a trough or small rock garden.*

Lewisia (Portulacaceae)

This is a genus which originates in the west of the United States in the rocky mountains of the national parks in California, Oregon, Nevada, and Washington, and British Columbia in Canada. There are species found in different habitats – on scree slopes, in alpine meadows, but also attached to protruding ledges in precarious positions, and even in semi-desert climates where the rainfall is seasonal and unpredictable.

Lewisia is usually easy to cultivate, but some are more difficult, which provides a challenge if you have already tried all the easy species. A hobby like this has endless possibilities. Most species are grown from seed.

Lewisia cotyledon makes strong, evergreen rosettes of leaves, which sometimes have crinkled or indented edges. The strong stalks carry many very beautiful pink flowers, sometimes striped or white-lipped. There are many hybrids. Give them a semi-shaded spot. They grow well in rock crevices and alpine houses. They reach about 30cm (12in) and like acid soil, but will also flourish on limestone.

L. rediviva is a species with both white and pink forms which flowers in May or June and whose rosette-forming leaves are shed as early as late summer. You must then give them less water because they are already starting their resting period. They grow well in an alpine house.

Lewisia brachycalix is a species which requires an instruction manual but is well worth the effort. In the winter it disappears, leaves and all, as with most perennials.

The white or pale pink flowers nestle in a rosette of sea-green leaves. In contrast to the other *Lewisia* species, this one flourishes in the sun on scree or otherwise in the alpine house.

Keep it moist in the spring and once it has died down just keep it slightly damp.

Lithodora diffusa (Boraginaceae)

Previously this plant was called *Lithospernum diffusum* and it is still found in some catalogues under this name. This plant is actually a sub-shrub, and is sometimes included with shrubs in one instance and with perennials in another.

It is a creeping, climbing plant which is usually no taller than 50cm (20in) depending on where it is placed. It has hairy, dark green leaves, and sky-blue flowers which appear from May to the end of July, and are very remarkable because of their wonderful colour.

It is advisable to prune it back after flowering. It is not totally hardy and can freeze completely in an unsheltered spot.

It requires acid or neutral ground and is therefore most suitable for troughs, containers or raised beds where you can include it among plants with the same requirements. The plant is propagated from seed, with cuttings from sturdy stems, or layering.

Cultivars of *Lithidora diffusa* include *L.d.* 'Alba' and *L.d.* 'Heavenly Blue'.

Lychnis (Caryophyllaceae)

This is a genus of summer-flowering annuals, biennials, and perennials of which only one species is grown in the rock garden. It likes porous soil and a sunny position.

It is propagated from seed or by division.

Lychnis alpina was previously called *Viscaria alpina* and is still found under that name. It is a bushy perennial which becomes covered with dark pink and occasionally white flowers in the summer.

It grows to about 15cm (6in) and has intensely green, dense foliage.

Meconopsis (Papaveraceae)

The smaller species of this genus can be used in the rock garden. For the most part they are perennials which seed themselves abundantly. They usually like a humus-rich soil and shade.

M. cambrica has vivid yellow and orange flowers and can become a weed.

M. horridula has lilac-purple flowers and dies off immediately after flowering.

Mertensia (Boraginaceae)

This genus has funnel-shaped flowers. It can grow in sunlight or shade, so long as there is very good, fairly deeply drained soil.

It can be propagated by division in the spring or from seed in the autumn.

M. echioides has hairy leaves and beautiful blue flowers. It likes a sunny position, and grows to a height of about 25cm (10in).

Moltkia (Boraginaceae)

A family of deciduous, semi-evergreen and evergreen plants and sub-shrubs which can be propagated from summer cuttings or seed.

Moltkia doerfleri has light purple

Sempervivum arachnoideum *in close-up.*

Opposite page: Gentiana septemfida *has lovely flowers.*

flowers throughout the summer. It is a bushy sub-shrub with narrow, greyish leaves. It grows to about 40cm (16in) tall and 30cm (12in) across and is completely hardy. It likes well-drained soil and grows on chalk and limestone rocks. *M.* x *intermedia* is a hybrid of *Moltkia suffruticosa.* It is a fully hardy, evergreen sub-shrub, growing about 30cm (12in) high and 50cm (20in) across. Masses of funnel-shaped, bright blue flowers appear in the summer. *Moltkia petraea* grows to about 30cm (12in) in height and spread, and has pink buds which open into pastel blue flowers in early summer.

The plant is completely hardy and can be propagated from seed or cuttings.
M. suffruticosa (*M. graminifolia*) is a deciduous, upright sub-shrub with clusters of funnel-shaped flowers in summer. The buds are initially pink and grow on hairy stalks. The plant grows 15-40cm (6in-16in) tall and 30cm (12in) across, and likes porous soil and a sunny position. It is completely hardy.

Morisia (Cruciferae)

This is a genus with only one species, *Morisia monanthos*. This is a perennial which is very suitable for the alpine house. It has bright yellow flowers in late spring and early summer and leathery, dark green foliage. It likes well-drained, gritty soil and is propagated by division of the roots.

Myosotis alpestris (Boraginaceae) – alpine forget-me-not

Although this is a short-lived forget-me-not it is hardy. It is at most 10-15cm (4-6in) high and as much across. It has azure blue flowers with a creamy-white heart. It likes direct sun and well-drained ground. Grow it from seed. It is found in alpine meadows and on rocks in the higher mountainous regions.

Omphalodes (Boraginaceae)

A genus of annuals and perennials which fit very well in the rock garden. They make a wonderful carpet and in the spring have forget-me-not coloured flowers which seem to wink at you from a distance. They grow very easily on any type of

Erigeron aureus *'Canary Bird' has golden yellow flowers.*

Left:
Gentiana angustifolia *is a plant for heavier soil.*

Opposite page:
Hepatica transsilvanica *'Flore Pena' is a beautiful double form.*

soil and *O. verna* and *O. cappadocica* flourish in half-shade as well as full shade.

They are easy to cultivate by division or from seed.

O. cappadocica is a perennial with creeping stems and sprays of little blue flowers which appear late in the spring. It grows about 15cm (6in) high.

O. verna is a plant that blooms in early spring, also with beautiful bright blue flowers.

It is slightly taller than the other species.

Onosma alborosea (Boraginaceae)

This is a very hairy perennial which produces semi-evergreen tussocks. Sometimes the hairs can irritate the skin.

It blooms in summer, with the white flowers turning pink.

It likes a sunny position and is very hardy. It grows to about 30cm (12in) high and 20cm (8in) across and flourishes best on well-drained, neutral or chalky soil.

It is suitable for walls and other warm situations.

Origanum (Labiatae) – dittany

O. vulgare (wild marjoram) is found throughout the whole of Europe on scree slopes and dry grasslands.

It is a sub-shrub which loses its leaves in the winter.

The plant has scented, dark green leaves, and small lilac-pink flowers during the summer.

It can be propagated by various methods– division, cuttings, and from seed – and is very easy to cultivate. It is a drooping plant which at about 45cm (18in) is rather tall for the rock garden.

O. amamum is more appropriate, growing 20cm (8in) high with pale pink to white flowers in summer.

It grows best in an alpine house, mainly because it dislikes humidity.

O. laevigatum grows well in a sunny, lime-rich site.

It produces an abundance of cherry-pink flowers and grows about 25cm (10in) tall.

O. rotundifolium is also a fairly low-growing sub-shrub.

Throughout the summer it is covered with pale pink flowers enclosed by greenish yellow bracts.

It flourishes in a sunny, chalky position.

O.r. 'Kent Beauty' is very attractive, but it is not very hardy.

Orostachys iwarenge (Crassulaceae)

This plant is sometimes called

Sedum iwarenge and originates in China.

It is not easy to cultivate, but its cream-coloured, torch-like flowers are very satisfying if you grow it in a very dry place outside or in the alpine house.

Parochetus (Leguminosae)

A genus with only one species, namely *Parochetus communis*.

It is suitable for the alpine greenhouse.

With its wonderful, evergreen, clover-like leaves, and tiny bright blue, flowers which are produced almost the whole year round, it is an unusual plant for damp, gritty ground.

It is about 5cm (2in) high and spreads out well. Propagation is by division and root runners. It is not too difficult to find.

Papaver (Papaveraceae) – poppy

This is a genus for sunny or semi-shaded spots of which most species are easy to sow.

There are annuals and biennials as well as perennials.

Papaver burseri (alpine poppy) is a semi-evergreen perennial which is short-lived.

It grows to about 20cm (8in) and is useful in the rock garden and on walls.

The flowers are white and appear throughout the summer.

P. miyabeanum has greenish-yellow flowers which emerge from a rosette of finely cut, hairy leaves.

P. nudicaule (Iceland poppy) seems to do very well in the rock garden if it has some shade.

The single flowers are either white or yellowish. It is summer-flowering.

Phlox (Polemoniaceae)

A genus of annuals and perennials that flower from late spring and throughout the summer with fabulous colours. They grow in fertile, fairly damp soil.

It is advisable to cut back plants in the rock garden after flowering.

They can be propagated from stem cuttings or seed.

Phlox adsurgens is an evergreen, carpeting plant which grows to about 15cm (6in).

Its stalks become woody on the underside and hold the oval, light to mid-green leaves.

In summer it bears clusters of short-stemmed, pink, violet, or white flowers.

It is suitable for a peat bed as well as the rock garden, because it likes a fairly peaty, acid soil. 'Wagon Wheel' is a pink cultivar.

P. bifida has small lilac or white flowers against a background of spear-shaped leaves and is not evergreen. Cut the stems back to half their length after flowering to keep a good shape. The plant is about 10cm (4in) tall.

A slightly taller species is *P. divaricata*, a semi-evergreen, creeping plant. During the summer it has pale to deep violet-blue flowers on stems with oval leaves.

There are many cultivars of the species *P. douglasii*, such as *P. douglasii* 'Boothman's Variety' with its lavender-blue flowers with violet centres. This is also evergreen and reaches about 5cm (2in). 'Crackerjack' has fuschia-coloured flowers and 'Red Admiral' is crimson.

P. procumbens is a 2.5cm (1in) high, evergreen plant with shiny, green foliage with white edges. The cerise-pink flowers appear in early summer.

P. stolonifera is an evergreen, creeping perennial, which is about 10cm (4in) high. It produces pale blue flowers early in the summer. This species likes damp, peaty, acid soil and is therefore ideal for the peat bed.

P. subulata is an evergreen perennial about 10cm (4in) tall. If it is in a sunny position it bears masses of white, pink or mauve flowers in early summer. There are various cultivars available of all the species mentioned, so you can create your own palette of colours.

Phuopsis stylosa (Rubiaceae)

This plant was previously called *Crucianella stylosa*.

It is a good ground-cover plant, especially for banks or in the rock garden.

It prefers a sunny, well-drained position. It is propagated from seed or half-ripe cuttings in the autumn.

Physoplexus (Campanulaceae)

This is a small genus with one species, *P. comosa*, also known as *Phyteuma comosum*.

It is a very beautiful perennial in cracks and crannies, with a remarkable display of pink and sometimes white flowers.

It is a very slow grower and dislikes wet winters.

It is a good plant to cultivate on limestone. It only grows to a height of about 10cm (4in).

Polygala (Polygalaceae) – milkwort

The milkwort genus contains shrubs or trees and some evergreen peren-

Thymus serpyllum *is an easy plant that is really worth growing.*

Right:
A close-up of Sedum acre *shows its attraction.*

Opposite page:
In this south-facing rock garden Raoulia *flowers abundantly.*

nials. Even annuals are included in it. Some of them are not completely hardy.

Polygala calcarea is an evergreen perennial with loose rosettes of narrow leaves and dark blue flowers in May and June.

It is a 2.5cm (1in) plant which likes humus-rich soil and thrives in a trough.

It is found in rocky, sandy, and chalky places.

P. chamaebuxus is evergreen and has dark green foliage on stalks which turn woody at the base.

The pea-like white and yellow flowers are sometimes tinted purple at the edges, and appear in late spring.

This plant also likes humus-rich soil and grows about 5cm (2in) tall.

It is very common in rocky parts of central Europe.

Polygonum (Polygonaceae) – knotweed

A genus of annuals and perennials, sometimes evergreen, which are not too difficult to cultivate. They can be grown from cuttings or seed.

Polygonum affine is an evergreen, mat–forming ground–cover plant which does not demand much from the soil. It is about 20cm (8in) tall and spreads out well.

The leaves are lancet-shaped and turn from green in the spring to bronze in the autumn. It flowers abundantly from early summer to late autumn.

P.a. 'Kew Form', a pinkish red cultivar of *Polygonum affine*, blooms in the summer.

P. vaccinniifolium is also known as *Persicaria vacciniifolia* or *Bistorta vacciniifolia*.

It is an evergreen, mat-forming plant with pretty red stalks bearing oval leaves. It blooms throughout the summer until well into the autumn, with small, pointed, deep red or pinkish-red flowers. It likes a humid position in full sun. It grows to about 20cm (8in) high and 30cm (12in) across, and is propagated by division or from seed.

Potentilla (Rosaceae)

In this genus there are numerous species which are important for the rock garden.

Potentilla crantzii, earlier known as *P. alpestris*, is a plant with dark green leaves and pale yellow flowers with an orange centre. The name "alpestris" indicates that it comes from the Alps, actually from the lower mountains and primarily from alpine meadows. It is about 10cm (4in) high. It is propagated by

sowing, division, and cuttings.

P. eriocarpa is a creeping variety, which grows about 5cm (2in) high and has oval, dark green, divided foliage. In the summer it bears flat, single, pale yellow flowers, which stand just above the foliage. This is a completely hardy species which likes full sun on well-drained soil. Propagate by seed, division, or cuttings.

P. nitida forms a compact mat with silvery, hairy foliage. It only grows to 5cm (2in) and produces light pink to white flowers with a dark centre in early summer. It likes chalky soil and is very suitable for the rock garden or a trough. Propagate by seed, cuttings, or division.

Pratia (Campanulaceae)

In this genus there is a species which can be grown in the alpine house, namely *Pratia angulata*. Its white, star-shaped flowers appear in May above narrow, dark green leaves, followed by purplish red fruit in the autumn.

It likes a humid position with some shade. Propagation is by seed or cuttings.

Primula (Primulaceae) – primrose

This is a large genus of rosette-forming plants.

They are subdivided into a number of groups which do not need to be mentioned here.

Here I shall limit myself to a few easily cultivated primulas.

You can use them practically anywhere – in the borders, the rock garden, the container, or the bog garden.

Primulas are at home anywhere, but they are not all quite so easy to cultivate.

In fact there are species which do not like a wet winter and that can be a problem.

Primulas are usually hardy but a few will die if the temperature drops to −10 C.

Some species can be grown from seed and the others by division or splitting.

Primula allionii only grows about 10cm (4in) tall. It is not completely hardy. It has pink, light purple or white tubular flowers. It likes direct sun or very light shade and friable, alkaline soil.

P. auricula grows on limestone rocks in the mountains. It is a perennial with aromatic, flat, green flowers and soft, oval, light green to greyish green leaves.

It likes direct sun or semi-shade and

Polygala calcarea *'Lillet' growing with* Daphne *x* thauma.

Right: A show form of Primula auricula

Opposite page:
Asplenium trichomanes *nestles in cracks on a wall.*

friable, sandy, alkaline soil. It is about 20cm (8in) tall.

P. clarkei likes some shade and peaty ground. It grows about 10cm (4in) high and in spring produces flat, pink flowers with a yellow centre. The flowers only just reach above the exquisite, light green leaves.

It is a completely hardy perennial.

P. clusiana is a perennial which is also completely hardy and produces pink, tubular flowers with a white centre, also in spring. It likes light shade to full sun and friable, peaty soil.

P. elatior is 20cm (8in) high and produces small, bell-shaped, fragrant yellow flowers that emerge from toothed green foliage in the spring. It likes a slightly peaty, moist soil and a sunny or slightly shaded position.

P. farinosa has bell-shaped, lilac pink and very occasionally white flowers in the spring and likes a slightly shaded or sunny position on peaty soil.

It is a completely hardy perennial. Its toothed leaves look as if they have been sprinkled with white flour. In the mountains it grows mainly in damp meadows and peaty places.

P. flaccida is a short-lived perennial which is also completely hardy and grows to about 30cm (12in).

It produces bell-shaped, hanging, lavender-coloured or violet flowers above its narrow, oval leaves in early summer.

Prunella (Labiatae) – self-heal
This is a genus of semi-evergreen perennials which produce pointed flowers in the summer.

They grow in the sun or shadow, and form good ground cover.

In the wild they are found on rocks and in woods.

They can be divided in the spring.

Prunella grandiflora is 10-15cm (4-6in) high and has light purple flowers.

Although it can become invasive, it provides lovely ground cover for the rock garden.

Trimming it back after flowering maintains a nicer shape.

P. vulgaris has vivid, blue-purple flowers on upright stems, which sometimes reach 30cm (12in) in height.

The plant spreads by means of short, creeping runners.

Alyssum wulfenianum *blooms in the summer with bright yellow flowers. It has small, grey leaves and grows about 20cm (8in) high.*

Right:
Dianthus plumarius *'White Hills' is a 10cm (4in) high plant with pink flowers that have a dark centre.*

Opposite page:
When you see Sedum acre *flowering beside a motorway crash barrier or on a grass verge, you can well imagine that it is not very demanding.*

Pterocephalus perennis (Dipsacaceae)

A semi-evergreen perennial which is mat-forming and has curled, hairy leaves. It has pinkish, single flowers on short stems in the summer. It is hardy and likes a sunny position on well-drained soil. It is a good rock plant and self seeds freely.

Pulsatilla (Ranunculaceae)

This is a family of perennials which normally produce a substantial number of large leaves.
So give them space in a large rock garden!
They have root-stocks which you can use to propagate them and sowing them is also possible if you use fresh seeds. The seed cases are beautiful, they are covered in silky hairs. Most *Pulsatilla* species do not like to be transplanted.

They like chalky soil, apart from *Pulsatilla. alpina* ssp. *apiifolia* and *P. vernalis*, which both prefer the soil to be more acid and so feel at home in a fairly damp peat bed.
P. alpina has feathery foliage and the white, sometimes blue or pink, nodding flowers appear in the spring. It is about 25cm (10in) tall.
P. alpina ssp. *apiifolia* has soft green foliage and bell-shaped, pale yellow flowers in the spring.
P. halleri, which is about 20cm (8in) tall, has lavender blue flowers above light green foliage.
I have seen *P. patens* at Wisley in August covered with gorgeous purple flowers.
P. vernalis is a bushy perennial with hairy, brown buds which appear in late winter.
These buds do not like wet winters so protection is recommended.

Ramonda (Gesneriaceae)

A genus of evergreen perennials with wrinkly, hairy foliage. They grow in the Pyrenees in crevices and on the shaded side of damp rocks. They can be propagated from leaf and root cuttings.
Ramonda myconi, also called *R. pyrenaica* in the catalogues, is a species with flat, blue, pink or white flowers which bloom in spring. The foliage is deeply wrinkled and on the underside it has dense, woolly, rust-coloured hairs.
It grows about 10cm (4in) high, and as with other *Ramonda* species it likes a position in the shade or semi-shade.
R. nathaliae is also 10cm (4in) high and in the spring has lavender-blue or white flowers with yellow anthers.
Its foliage is pale green.

R. serbica looks like *R. nathaliae* but it has lilac-blue flowers with dark violet anthers and is more difficult to grow.

Raoulia (Compositae)

A family of evergreen, mat-forming plants which are cultivated for their foliage. They are perennials which are suited to the alpine house, troughs, or rock gardens.
They need gritty, peaty soil and they like semi-shade.
They can be propagated from cuttings or seed.
Raoulia australis is a plant which forms a carpet with greyish-green leaves. The sulphur yellow flowers appear in summer. It is only about 1cm (1/3in) high but has a spread of about 25cm (10in).
R. hookeri produces rosettes of silver-coloured foliage. It prefers a

situation in an alpine house in dry, gritty soil.
This plant also has small, yellow flowers in summer.

Sagina (Carophyllaceae)

A genus of mat-forming plants, including annuals and evergreen perennials, which are cultivated for their foliage.
The plants are very suitable for use between paving slabs.
They are very attractive planted on a terrace.
Try not to put them in a very warm, dry place. They are easily propagated by division in the spring or from seed in the autumn.
Sagina boydii is an evergreen, ground-covering perennial which grows quite slowly and can be propagated from cuttings.
Its flowers are not very remarkable

but that makes its stiff, dark green leaves all the more noticeable.
S. subulata looks like a flowering moss with its small, white flowers. There are a few cultivars available which are worth mentioning – 'Aurea' has yellow mossy cushions, and 'Senior' is a coarser, untidy plant.

Saponaria (Carophyllaceae) – soapwort

In this genus of fairly invasive perennials and a few annuals, there are some species which are suitable for the rock garden, a scree slope, or bank. They very much like well-drained soil and a sunny position. They are propagated from seed in the spring or cuttings in the early summer. The best known variety is *S. ocymoides*, a creeping soapwort which produces delicate pink flow-

In the rock garden at the University of Utrecht there is a good collection of ferns.
Right: Pulsatilla halleri *resembles other members of the genus* Pulsatilla *with its hairy, silver seed heads.*
Opposite page: Saxifraga longifolia *comes from the Pyrenees.*

ers in late spring. This perennial is excellent in a dry place. From the cultivars I can recommend the white 'Alba' and 'Rubra Compacta'. The latter is not completely hardy, so it is better placed in a greenhouse. *Saponaria* x *olivana* is a sub-species of *S. caespitosa* and is also a perennial, which produces pale pink flowers in the summer. It must have very well-drained soil. It grows about 10cm (4in) high and forms cushions of stiff, green, oval leaves.

Saxifraga (Saxifragaceae) – saxifrage

This is one of the largest and most important genus for rock gardens, raised beds, pots, troughs, dishes, and the alpine house. The plants are usually hardy. They can be propagated from seed or root cuttings.

Saxifrages can be divided into four groups: group 1 includes species which have to be protected from over-damp soil and midday sun; group 2 includes species which need to stand in semi-shade and well-drained soil; group 3 includes species which do not like dry roots. Most species in this group form cushions and flower in the early spring on stems which are barely visible above the leaves.
Finally, group 4 includes the species which require full sun and well-drained, alkaline soil, most of which have hard leaves. The saxifrages can be further subdivided according to their manner of cultivation.
Then there are mossy species, cushion-forming species or Kabschias and the bell saxifrages or Englerias, and those with silver leaves in rosettes.

Here I will only discuss the species which are not too difficult to grow. There are many species available and, if your hobby threatens to develop into an art form, then you would be well advised to buy a book which goes into more detail about the saxifrage genus.
S. burseriana is about 5cm (2in) high and belongs to the group of cushion-forming species.
It is a slow-growing evergreen, which produces white flowers on short red stalks in the spring.
The foliage is grey-green.
The plant is cultivated as in group 3 and it is hardy.
S. fortunei (syn. *S. cortusifolia* var. *fortunei*) is an evergreen perennial with green to brownish-green leaves.
It blooms in autumn with a cloud of little white flowers.

S.f. 'Rubrifolia' produces its flowers on dark red stalks and has dark red and green leaves with bright red undersides.

It belongs to group 1.

S. cuneifolia which has white flowers and reaches about 15cm (6in) high, is a native of mountain forests and shaded places.

From May throughout the summer, it produces small, white flowers which sometimes have yellow, pink, or red spots.

This species does not fit into any of the groups, but it is an excellent rock plant or border plant.

It likes moist ground and is very hardy.

It is cultivated like plants in group 1.

S. longifolia has white flowers on long stems.

Unfortunately, for this plant flowering means certain death because it is monocarpic. This term is used for perennials (not for an annual or biennial) which seed once and then die.

It is possible that it has been growing for a number of years before it flowers.

S. longifolia belongs to the group with silver rosettes and is cultivated as group 4.

S. paniculata (syn. *S. aizoon*) is a 15-25cm (6-10in) plant which belongs to the group with silver rosettes and is an evergreen, completely hardy perennial.

At the start of summer it produces mostly white, round flowers.

In the wild it grows on rocks and scree slopes.

The white cultivar 'Minor' only grows about 4in (10cm) high.

S. paniculata and *S.p.* 'Minor' are treated as the plants in group 4.

This plant, sometimes known as Sedum iwarenge, *but actually* Orostachys iwarenge, *belongs to the family* Crassulaceae.

Opposite page: Physoplexis comosa *is an intriguing plant from the Dolomites.*

Scutellaria (Labiatae) – skullcap

This is a genus of summer-flowering perennials with root-stocks and with the lip flowers characteristic of the labiates.

The plants like a sunny place and are propagated by division or from seed.

Scutellaria alpina produces abundant blue-purple flowers on top of pale leaf bracts in June to July.

The plant is about 15cm (6in) tall.

S. orientalis has yellow-green flowers with a brown lip in June and July. These hairy plants with greyish stems are about 10cm (4in) high.

Sedum (Crassulaceae) – stonecrop

These plants often have fleshy leaves. The genus includes perennials, annuals, biennials, shrubs, and sub-shrubs.

Usually they are evergreen or sometimes semi-evergreen.

They are very suitable plants for rock gardens. They are easily divided, but you cean also propagate *Sedum* from stem cuttings.

Sedum acre (biting stonecrop) is found throughout Europe on rocks and walls.

It is an evergreen, mat-forming plant with fleshy leaves and bright yellow, stellate flowers in the summer.

It spreads very easily, but that is not a problem because it is easy to weed out again. It is about 2.5cm (1in) high.

S. anacampseros is a semi-evergreen perennial which spends the winter with leaf rosettes above the ground. It grows about 10cm (4in) high with a spread of 25cm (10in) or more. It is completely hardy and has purple-pink flowers in the summer which grow on brown stalks with fleshy, green leaves.

It is easily grown from seed and can also be layered. It is very suitable for the rock garden.

S. kamtschaticum has yellow flowers in the summer and remains partly green in the winter.

The foliage is fleshy and the plant is about 5cm (2in) high.

S. sempervivoides is an evergreen biennial. In some ways the rosettes resemble those of *Sempervivum*. The flowers which appear in the summer are scarlet.

S. spurium has pretty pink flowers in summer. It is an easily cultivated creeping perennial.

Sempervivum (Crassulaceae) – houseleek

Houseleeks are evergreen perennials which form lovely rosettes of fleshy leaves. They can be used in various ways in the rock garden– on scree slopes, in containers and dishes, but also in the alpine house. They are very easy to hybridize, they like the sun and can be propagated from runners.

There are many species for sale.

Sempervivum arachnoideum (the cobweb houseleek) is very beautiful. The plant is worth cultivating for the network of cobweb-like hairs on the fleshy, red-tipped leaves and the rose-like carmine flowers which appear from July to September.

It is about 10cm (4in) high and likes to be in full sun.

It grows in mountainous regions, on rocks, scree slopes, and walls.

Just to make your mouth water – a close-up of Gentiana angustifolia.

Left: Erigeron karvinskianus, *a fleabane that flowers profusely and for a long time, with pink flowers turning white later. It is suitable for walls, even though it is not totally hardy.*

Opposite page: The round cushions of Acantholimon *look good anywhere.*

S. tectorum is the common house-leek, with rosettes of stiff, pointed, blue-green and sometimes red-tinged leaves. The rosettes do not grow higher than 5cm (2in), while the strong flower stems can tower up to 40cm (16in). The flower stems support pale red flowers.

In addition there are S. *ciliosum*, which does not like damp winters and is therefore better off in the alpine house, and S. *montanum*, which grows on rocks in mountainous regions and has beautiful, brownish-green rosettes.

This species is quite variable.

Silene (Caryophyllaceae) – campion

There are both annuals and perennials in this genus, some of which are evergreen.

They are grown for their mass of flowers but not all species are hardy. They like well-drained, fertile soil and a sunny position.

They can be propagated from seed in spring or autumn, or from cuttings.

Silene acaulis (moss campion) is a bright green, cushion-forming, mossy perennial from the polar and alpine regions.

It produces pink flowers in the spring and because of its origins it likes a cool climate.

It is a very suitable plant for rock crevices and a damp spot in the rock garden. It does not grow any higher than 2.5cm (1in).

S. *elisabethae* is a perennial which produces rosettes of medium green leaves, out of which dark pink flowers with a green centre appear in summer.

The plant is most suitable if you can keep it under control, either in a trough or a container.

S. *schafta* has fuschia-coloured flowers on stalks with oval leaves. It grows about 15cm (6in) tall and 10cm (4in) across.

Silene vulgaris ssp. *maritima* is an attractive plant, growing up to 20cm (8in) tall.

It has white, pompom flowers on greyish-green stems with greyish-green, spear-shaped leaves.

Sisyrinchium (Iridaceae)

The members of this genus like well-drained or damp soil and a position in full sun or semi-shade. They can be easily be divided or grown from seed. *Sisyrinchium graminoides* (syn. *S. angustifolium*) produces blue flowers with a yellow centre throughout the summer. It originates in North America but now it is

found in many parts of Europe, including alpine meadows.

Its height and spread are about 20cm (8in). *S. bermudiana* has similar flowers to *S. graminoides* but flowers in the spring until early summer and grows to about 30cm (12in) in height.

S. californicum is a yellow-flowered, semi-evergreen plant which can grow to about 30cm (12in). It blooms from late spring until the middle of summer and its flower heads are quite large, up to 2.5cm (1in) across.

S. macounii (syn. *S. idahoense*) has cup-shaped purple flowers in the spring and summer. There is also a white cultivar, 'Album'.

Solidago (Compositae) – golden rod

Most members of this genus are not suitable for the rock garden because they are too tall.

One species is quite small, *Solidago virgaurea* var. *minutissima* which is only about 10cm (4in).

I find it attractive because it only reveals its yellow flowers in the autumn.

It is very suitable for the rock garden, a trough, or the alpine house. Propagate by division.

Teucrium (Labiatae)

A genus which includes evergreens, deciduous shrubs, sub-shrubs, and perennials.

I find only *Teucrium montanum* suitable for the rock garden or a scree slope.

This is a ground-covering perennial with quite woody stalks.

It produces whitish to yellow flowers from May to August.

Thymus (Labiatae) – thyme

This is a genus of evergreen, ground-covering plants with fragrant foliage.

They are used as culinary herbs, but they also provide ideal ground cover in the rock garden. They are not always fully hardy, but you cannot imagine any garden without thyme. *Thymus serpyllum* is the wild thyme which is appreciated for its scented leaves, creeping twigs, and upright stems. Its flowers make a picturesque pink carpet from May to August.

In the wild, this thyme grows on dry hillocks and in forested places throughout Europe.

Townsendia (Compositae)

These are short-lived plants with beautiful, daisy-like flowers. They are suitable for the alpine

Onosma taurica *comes from the Taurus mountains in Turkey.*

Left:
Helichrysum frigidum, *like related species, looks beautiful in the rock garden.*

house, because however much they dislike our damp winters, they still appreciate some humidity.

They are propagated from seed.

Townsendia grandiflora has violet flowers in May to June and is only 15cm (6in) tall.

T. parryi is an evergreen, rosette-forming perennial which again grows up to 15cm (6in) tall.

The lavender-blue flowers with a yellow centre appear in May above the spoon-shaped foliage.

Waldsteinia ternata (Rosaceae)

A creeping, rather invasive semi-evergreen, ground-covering perennial.

Its yellow flowers appear in late spring and early summer.

It is hardy and likes full sun and well-drained soil. It can be divided in early spring.

Ferns

In the mountains there are also ferns in rocky and peaty places. Although they do not have flowers, they should not be ignored if you are planning a rock garden.

Just a few of the many ferns which can be included in a rock garden are mentioned here.

Adianthum pedatum (northern maidenhair fern) comes from North America and is a small fern which grows about 40cm (16in) tall.

It likes shade and is not hardy everywhere, but in a sheltered spot it will give you a lot of pleasure.

Adiantum venustum, a deciduous fern from the Himalayas, grows well on walls with its light green leaves.

Asplenium ruta-muraria (wall rue), which is commonly found on old town walls and church towers, is a sun-loving fern.

Its relative, *Asplenium trichomanes* (maidenhair spleenwort), is planted more often in rock gardens. It fares very well on walls, in sunlight, or shadow. *Blechnum penna-marina*, is a fairly short variety which grows quite quickly to a height of about 30cm (12in) and is suitable for crevices and rock gardens. *Ceterach officinarum* (rusty-back fern) likes lime-rich soil. It is also often found in rock crevices. A position with some sun suits it.

Matteucia struthiopteris (ostrich fern) fits in well on the shaded side of a rock garden. It is a large fern with fresh green foliage. Keep an eye on it because before you know it, your garden will be filled with *Matteucia*. Members of the genus *Polystichum*, and their various cultivars also grow well in the shaded parts of the larger rock garden.

Bulbs and tubers

Judging by the number of catalogues that

come through the letter box it would seem that flower bulbs have become very fashionable during the last few years.

Previously, there were only the usual ones such as tulip, hyacinth, and crocus, but now there are many new and exotic varieties available.

Some of these new varieties of bulbs and tubers are well-suited to the rock garden.
A large selection of these colourful plants can also be grown in pots, trays, troughs, and raised beds.

Tulipa clusiana *is a rare tulip that shows its true colours in good sunlight.*

Only the varieties of the *Allium* (onion) family that do not seed themselves too profusely are recommended. *Allium cernuum*, a gorgeous, red-and white-flowering, decorative onion with drooping flowers, is not to be missed.
A. narcissiflorum is definitely worth the effort for its pinkish red flowers and grey-green leaves.
Also worth planting are *A. moly*, a yellow decorative onion that seeds itself profusely, and *A. oreophilum*, a carmine red species.

Bulbocodium vernum is a bulbous plant found in the Caucasus, the Balkans, and the Alps.
It starts to flower very early and you might see the reddish-purple flowers in January.
This plant enjoys a sunny position and well-drained soil.

It is nice to set *Chionodoxa* in groups to display the pretty blue flowers that bloom in early spring at their best. It seeds itself, but is also easy to weed out.

There are many species of *Colchicum*, one of which is the autumn-flowering meadow saffron or so-called "autumn crocus".

Look at the catalogues of various bulb growers, where there are detailed descriptions of the different bulb species that also mention their origins.

Colchicum resembles a crocus, but from close up there are some differences.

Crocusses, *Crocus*, always add something to a garden, in every size or variety. They bloom in the spring and autumn when there are few other flowers. They are best placed under and around bedding plants, where their ugly dying leaves are less visible.

Cyclamen are tuberous plants which also flower in spring and autumn. They flourish best in a shaded position which is not too damp. The easy species to grow are *C. hederifolium*, which produces pale to deep pink flowers from August onwards, and *C. coum*, whose dark red to carmine red flowers appear in January. *C. cilicium* is also recommended for its pink flowers and marbled leaves.

Erythronium is a tuberous plant that has been well known for a long time. In particular, *Erythronium dens-canis* (dog's tooth violet) has been grown for centuries. Unfortunately it is a rather difficult plant–

Galanthus nivalis 'Flore Pleno' is a double snowdrop that is excellent in a rock-garden.

the bulbs can quickly dry out after lifting. There are many species of *Erythronium* available, and every one of them is worth considering.

Not all species of *Fritillaria* are suitable for the rock garden. For example, the enormous crown imperial is simply too tall.
However, in my opinion, the speckled flowers of *Fritillaria meleagris* (the snake's-head fritillary), and the wonderful reddish purple flowers of *F. michailovskyi* are wonderful additions to the rock garden if it is planted in a slightly shaded position.

The snowdrop, *Galanthus*, is also ideal in the rock garden. There is nothing so lovely as to see the first snowdrop emerging through a blanket of snow. There are also other species of this bulb available.

From the *Iris* family I will only mention *Iris reticulata*, which smells lovely and is so easy to grow. There are beautiful hybrids of this bulb that grow to a maximum of 20cm (8in) high. They flower throughout March in a sunny position.

The summer snowflake, *Leucojum vernum*, can be planted in a damp part of the rock garden, like *L. autumnale*.
This small, winter-flowering species has tiny, white bell-shaped flowers, with a hint of pink.

Allium flavum *from close up. The colour is particularly striking.*

Following pages:
Iris danfordiae *is a species which has golden yellow flowers in March.*

99

The *Muscari*, or grape hyacinth, is recognized by everyone, but few people know that as well as the common species, there are also some with short heads of flowers. There are also white cultivars.

Muscari armeniacum is not uncommon, but *M. azureum* and *M. azureum* 'Album' are more unusual. They tend not to spread as rapidly.

Crown imperial, Fritillaria imperialis *'Lutea', is an eye-catching addition to a larger rock garden, although it is more commonly seen in borders.*

It is obvious that the normal, large-flowered daffodils, *Narcissus*, do not belong in the rock garden. There are, however, a number of attractive, small-flowered species which stay small and have very nice shapes, different from the typical form. *Narcissus bulbocodium* (hoop-petticoat daffodil) is a good choice. Put *N. asturiensis* on your list, too. It grows only 10cm (4in) high and is in flower as early as February. Other species are *N. cernuus* and *N. minor* both of which prefer some humidity.

Rhodohypoxis baurii belongs to a genus of dwarf, spring- and summer-flowering tubers. They mostly have red, pink or white flowers. They are not completely hardy and therefore most suitable for a cold frame or greenhouse.

They grow best in peaty soil, which must be kept damp while they are flowering. It is, however, better to keep them dry during the winter. They can be grown from seed.

Perhaps Leucojum vernum *does not belong in the rock garden itself, but growing in a peat bed to announce the arrival of spring.*

Among the species of *Scilla*, *Scilla bifolia* produces wonderfully scented, pretty blue flowers. Some gardeners regard it as rather too invasive. *S. litardierei* is also recommended. This plant grows to about 15cm (6in) and flowers in May or June.

Only the short species of *Tulipa* should be used. Simply plant the tall varieties elsewhere in the garden and keep the less well-known species for the rock garden.
Tulipa biflora is a nice variety that only grows to 12cm (5in) in height and has fragrant white flowers.
The 15cm (6in) species, *T. maximowiczii*, blooms in April or May with bright red flowers with a blue-black centre.
I should also mention *T. tarda*, a famous, artificially cultivated tulip with yellow and white flowers.
T. turkestanica has greyish-green leaves and has yellow-hearted, creamy white flowers in February or March.

Rhodohypoxis baurii
'Fred Broome' is a
good cultivar.

Shrubs and trees

You will probably be surprised that there is a chapter about shrubs and trees in a book about rock gardens.

In fact, there are various species that are suitable for the rock garden, which I shall discuss here.

Despite the fact that there are very lovely trees and shrubs that fit superbly, in most rock gardens there are usually only perennials and bulbs.

If you talk to the owners of rock gardens, it seems that some of them are plant fanatics who do not even consider a tree or shrub to be a plant. Perhaps they know too little about shrubs and trees, or consider them to be too labour-intensive.

Trees and shrubs have to be pruned regularly and most people find this a nuisance.

People think pruning is difficult and it is also considered a waste of time. However, if you want to prevent your rock garden from being totally overrun then you will have to pick up the shears. The plants usually respond very well. They then grow sturdier branches and, though it might seem strange, it is usually a healthy stimulation for root growth, so there will be a better network under the soil too.

This is very beneficial for the plant. The shrubs and trees that are planted in the rock garden are not fast-growing.

When you have read the descriptions that follow, you will realize that most of them are very slow-growing and so pruning does not need to be drastic. It is usually achieved with a small piece of branch here and there. The timing of pruning depends on the type of plant.

Trees are usually pruned in winter. With shrubs you do have to use your common sense.

This "witche's broom" larch (Larix) *is a rarity. The knot in the lower stem reduces the flow of sap.*

There are a couple of rules, and if you follow these you will notice that growth carries on as normal and the shrub will not wither away if you cut off a branch.

Abies koreana 'Silber Kugel' is a slow-growing conifer with silver-coloured needles.

Pruning Shrubs which flower after 1 July do so on that year's sapwood or growth. You can prune these shrubs in March. Wait until the end of March because there could still be a hard frost.

Shrubs which flower before 1 July do so on the wood from the previous year's growth, so this type of shrub must be pruned after flowering.

Usually you have to remove all the flowering branches.

The plant can carry on growing immediately after that and still has a reasonable period of time to grow new wood for next year's flowers before the winter really sets in.

If the shrub has berries after flowering then it is a shame to prune all the flower heads because then you remove all the berries.

Remove a few of the branches from these shrubs to give them a good shape.

As I have already mentioned, the shrubs for the rock garden grow so slowly that it is only a question of removing small sections of branch, not whole ones.

Evergreen shrubs and conifers are best pruned in August, and it is better to wait for a rainy or damp day.

They are producing shoots less vigorously than in spring, which is when the plants grow most rapidly. Think, for example, of *Buxus*, the boxwood, which remains "neat" for longer if you cut it back in August, rather than in spring.

With rhododendrons and azaleas the larger kinds are pruned very sparingly. Just the odd twig that grows outside the main outline of the bush is removed.

Varieties for the rock garden thus require very little pruning. Just do enough to maintain their shape.

Deciduous shrubs and trees

There are many species or cultivars of the *Acer* (Aceraceae), or maple family, which are suitable for the rock garden. Most of the maples are trees, but *A. palmatum* has a number of cultivars which are very slow-growing and resemble shrubs. The non-green species do not like the early morning sun because they can scorch. The maples do not like being exposed to a cold wind.

In Edinburgh I saw an example of *A. palmatum* 'Butterfly', which has grey-green leaves with a cream-and pink-coloured border. It is a slow grower, at most 1m (3ft) tall. The purple flowers appear in the spring. As with the rest of the maples, it prefers a semi-shaded position and well-drained soil.

The name of the variety *A. palmatum* 'Red Pygmy' tells you that it is a dwarf maple. It has an attractive red leaf.

Syringa meyeri 'Palibin' is a favourite shrub for every garden.

Opposite page: Conifers and dwarf shrubs determine the structure of the rock garden.

106

Berberis thunbergii 'Atropurpurea Nana' *(Berberidaceae)* is a deciduous shrub which has pretty, reddish purple leaves on arching branches.

All barberry bushes have thorns on their branches, making them very suitable for planting in public gardens. In fact they are so suitable that few people want to have them in their gardens any more, but they are very attractive shrubs for the rock garden.

Betula nana (Betulaceae) is a birch that does not grow into a tree but becomes a branched, bushy, dwarf shrub, about 60cm (2ft) tall. It has small, toothed leaves that turn a gorgeous yellow colour in the autumn. The small yellow-brown catkins appear in the spring.

Cotoneaster horizontalis (Rosaceae), wall-spray, is a carpeting shrub that can be pruned easily and thus can be placed in the rock garden. It has bright red fruit, which makes it very attractive in the autumn.

Cytisus beanii (Leguminosae), a deciduous, low-growing, hardy shrub is excellent for use in the rock garden. Its golden yellow blossoms appear in late spring and early summer on long tendril-like branches from the previous year's wood. The tripartite leaves are small and hairy.

Cassiope *'Muirhead' with bell-shaped white flowers only grows to about 20cm (8in).*

The bush grows about 15cm (6in) tall and wide, and it likes a sunny position. *Cytisus decumbens* is likewise a low-growing broom species that does very well in the rock garden. With its abundance of yellow blossoms in late spring, it makes a striking feature. Its branches grow along the ground and in this way they can cover a piece of rock wonderfully.

C. purpureus (syn. *Chamaecytisus purpureus*), purple broom, and the white cultivar 'Albus' are somewhat taller bushes, growing to about 40cm (16in). *C. purpureus* has purple blossoms that grow on the previous year's wood in the early summer. This broom is also a sun-lover and is completely hardy.

Genista lydia (Leguminosae) is a nice, thornless gorse that displays its vivid yellow blossom on long curved branches.
It is beautiful if trained over a wall or a large piece of rock. It does like sun and good drainage. It grows to about 50cm (20in).
Genista sagittalis (syn. *Chamaespartium sagittale*) is also a thornless shrub with winged branches on which there are just a few oval, dark green leaves. In the early summer it has yellow blossom that grows close together in tight clusters. This is followed by hairy seed pods. It only grows about 10cm (4in) high, and it enjoys the sun.
In the wild it is found throughout the mountainous regions of central and southern Europe as far north as Belgium.

Daphne arbuscula looks splendid in the garden.

109

Petrophyton caespitosum (Rosaceae) is a mat-forming, evergreen shrub that is primarily grown for its pretty, small flowers in summer. It has hairy foliage and only grows 10cm (4in) high. It can spread to about 50cm (20in) across and is most suited for growing on limestone or in a cold frame.

It is hardy, but difficult to grow. It likes porous, lime-rich earth.

The difficulty with this plant is the high likelihood of attack by red spider mite and aphids in warm weather. It can be propagated from seed or half-ripe cuttings.

This white cultivar of Daphne cneorum is called 'Album' and is a lovely shrub that dislikes being transplanted as much as the other Daphne species.

Rhamnus pumilus (Rhamnaceae), the dwarf buckthorn, grows on the scree slopes and rocks high in the mountains.

It is a low, spreading, strongly branched shrub which creeps along the ground. In May or June, yellowish flower heads appear at the base of the young, thorned branches.

These are unisexual, which means the flowers have either stamens or pistils. It may not be easily available.

Various members of the willow family *(Salicaceae)* are suitable for the rock garden. The willow is a deciduous shrub that is so popular because of its very beautiful catkins, which are usually silver-grey in colour and covered in down.

Salix apoda is a slow-growing willow with thick, silky, silver-coloured catkins with orange to yellow stamens and pistils in the early summer. It has leathery foliage that is hairy when the shrub is young, turning a dark green colour later on. It grows about 20cm (8in) tall. *Salix x boydii* is a slow-growing, bushy shrub which is a natural hybrid. It has lovely, grey, deeply wrinkled leaves and it is one of the few willows which almost never produces catkins. It grows about 25cm (20in) tall and 40cm (16in) wide. It is hardy and prefers quite damp soil. In the spring, S. *helvetica* has silky, grey catkins on short stalks, which turn yellow later in the year. It is a shrub which grows so many branches that it gives a rather tangled impression, which is actually why it so attractive. As with most other willows it likes a damp position. S. *reticulata* is a stunning, slow-growing, cushion-forming willow that has red-brown catkins in the spring, turning yellow later. It has lovely, somewhat wrinkled leaves.

This shrub rarely grows taller than 5-8cm (2-3in) and particularly likes a cool position on damp soil.

From the mountain ash or rowan family there is only one species which is not terribly difficult to grow; that is *Sorbus reducta (Rosaceae)* with its pretty bronze-red, autumn colour. It is a shrub about 50cm (20in) tall and produces the familiar mountain ash foliage and flat white flowers that turns into rose-red berries. To grow to its full potential it needs quite a lot of sun.

Another beautiful Daphne *for the rock garden is* Daphne tangutica.

One of the *Stephanandra (Rosaceae)* cultivars that is suitable for the rock garden is *Stephanandra incisa* 'Crispa'. It grows about 50cm (20in) high and is actually a creeper. The foliage is quite deeply lobed.

Syringa meyeri 'Palibin' *(Oleaceae)* is a lovely, fragrant little shrub, which I often recommend to people. It is a shrub that you simply must have. Its lovely scent, its beautiful shape, and its slow growth make it very suitable for the rock garden.

It grows to about 1.5m (5ft) and flowers abundantly in May or June with single-flowered, lilac-pink blossom. It has small, oval, dark green leaves.

Syringa vulgaris is found in rocky regions of southern Europe and in May or June produces fragrant lilac-purple blossom.

The lower stem of this plant has been grafted with another variety to create the cultivar 'Uncle Tom'. It remains quite small but has normal foliage.

The elms are also a small, slow-growing type that we can utilize.

Most elms, which are very hardy and not unusual in a large garden, are tall trees, so we do not immediately think of this genus for the rock garden.

Ulmus hollandica 'Jacqueline Hillier' *(Ulmaceae)* is, however, a slow-growing, bushy shrub that eventually grows to a height of 2m

Larix decidua 'Vacikov' is a Czech form of the witche's broom larch.

(6ft) and with some pruning can be very well trained. The leaves have quite a rough texture and remain on the tree during winter.

Evergreen shrubs and trees

Andromeda needs a somewhat acid soil, so like all the *Ericaceae* is suitable for a peat bed. It can be propagated from cuttings or seed. *Andromeda polifolia* is an evergreen shrub with pink bottle-shaped flowers which appear in spring and early summer on hairless stems. The shrub grows about 40cm (16in) tall.

A.p. 'Alba' has white flowers and grows to the same height.

A.p. 'Compacta' is a smaller plant, growing about 25cm (10in) tall, also with pink flowers.

The bearberry, *Arctostaphylos uvaursi (Ericaceae)* is an evergreen shrub which likes a sunny position on acid ground. In the mountains it grows on rocks and peat. It has leathery foliage and pinkish white flowers. It is about 10cm (3in) high. 'Vancouver Jade' is a wonderful cultivar with white flowers in summer.

Berberis stenophylla 'Corallina Compacta' *(Berberidaceae)*, the barberry, is a dwarf shrub with thorn-covered branches and small, narrow leaves. In late spring it is covered in bright yellow-orange flowers. It grows very slowly and is difficult to propagate. It grows no more than 10in (25cm) tall and prefers to occupy a sunny position.

Pinus mugo 'Mini Mops' grows in a spherical form.

Cassiope (Ericaceae) is a spring-flowering, evergreen shrub which is suitable for peat beds and the rock garden. It prefers a sheltered, rather shaded situation and damp, acid soil. It can be propagated from cuttings or seed.

Cassiope 'Edinburgh' is a dwarf form with white blossom. *Cassiope lycopodioides* is also small, about 10cm (3in), and also has white blossom and dark green foliage. *C. mertensiana* is a little taller, about 15cm (6in), and has creamy-white flowers with green or red calyces.

From the *Cornus (Cornaceae)*, the dogwood family, I will only mention the ground-covering *Cornus canadensis*, the creeping dogwood, which has wonderful foliage and greenish-white blossom in the spring, followed by red berries. It is about 10cm (4in) high and likes slightly acid soil in a semi-shaded position.

Daphne (Thymelaceae) is a genus of evergreen and semi-evergreen shrubs, whose smaller varieties are very suitable for the rock garden. The seeds are poisonous. *Daphne alpina* has twisted, woolly, fragile branches and white, sweet-scented blossom. It grows on rocks and scree slopes in the mountains. *D. blagayana* grows mainly in the mountains of south-eastern Europe and has very fragrant, white to creamy-white blossom.

D. cneorum grows on rocks and meadows in the Alps and is a low,

Picea abies 'Acrocona Nana' is a dwarf variety of P.a. *'Acrocona'. The eight-year-old plant in the photograph is a mere 15cm (6in) tall.*

spreading shrub with beautifully scented blossom in pinkish-red bunches that appear in late spring. *D. jasminea* is a compact shrub about 10cm (3in) high whose pink blossom appears in late spring and then again in the autumn.

Rhododendron ferrugineum has dark pink to red flowers.

Erinacea anthyllis (Leguminosae), hedgehog broom, is a thorny, cushion-forming shrub that grows very slowly. It has tough, blue-green foliage and blue-violet flowers. It is not completely hardy and needs to be placed in a cold frame.

Gaultheria (Ericaceae) is a shrub for the peat bed and is grown for its foliage, flowers, and fruit.
It likes damp, peaty soil, and a place in the shade. It can be propagated from seed or cuttings.
Gaultheria cuneata has beautiful white flowers in the summer followed by white berries. It grows about 30cm (12in) tall.
G. procumbens is shorter, only about 15cm (6in) tall, with pink flowers and red berries. The leathery foliage turns a pretty red in winter.

Hedera (Araliaceae), the ivy, grows on walls and rocks in the shade. There are a number of cultivars, especially of the species *Hedera helix*, from this genus that are suitable for troughs, containers, and the rock garden.

115

Hedera is an evergreen plant that flourishes in all sorts of places in the garden once it has established itself.

There are also dwarf forms for the rock garden and larger types that make excellent ground cover. You can propagate them easily from cuttings or by layering. The cultivar 'Conglomerata' has small, curly leaves and is useful for small walls.

'Ivalace' is a small-growing variety with beautifully shaped, dark green foliage.

Kalmiopsis leachiana (Ericaceae) is an evergreen shrub that is very suitable for a peat bed. It likes acid, peaty soil, and some shade. It can be propagated from cuttings.

Loiseleuria procumbens (Ericaceae), trailing azalea, is a small, evergreen, creeping shrub with clusters of pinkish red flowers. It grows in meadows and on rocks in the arctic and alpine regions. It likes acid soil rich in humus and is quite difficult to cultivate. It can be propagated from cuttings or seed.

Phyllodoce (Ericaceae) is a low shrub about 30cm (12in) tall, with heather-like foliage and attractive flowers in spring. It likes a semi-shaded spot, and is propagated from seed or cuttings. *Phyllodoce aleutica* has greenish-white flowers and forms a carpet.

Kalmiopsis leachiana *is ideal for a peat bed. It is a member of the* Ericacae *family that is equally at home in a heather garden.*

P. caerulea has nodding, purple-coloured flowers on thin, reddish stems. *P. empetriformis* has dark pink flowers above a carpet.

Rhododendron (Ericaceae) is a genus of acid-loving, evergreen shrubs of which the dwarf species are suitable for peat beds and the rock garden. *Rhododendron ferrugineum* grows in acid mountain meadows and on rocks. It is an evergreen that grows 1m (3ft) high at the most.
It looks like an azalea but has leaves which are rust-coloured on the underside.
The flowers are a vivid pinkish red. The shrub is poisonous and was previously used as a medicine. *R. hirsutum* is similar to the previous species, but has foliage which is bright green on the underside as well as the upper side. It mainly grows on lime-rich soil in the Alps. This is the only rhododendron which does not prefer an acid soil.

Although *Vaccinium (Ericaceae)* is not always considered among the rock plants I will mention one species, *Vaccinium vitisidaea*, the cowberry, whose natural habitat is the mountain meadows. It is an evergreen, carpet-forming sub-shrub which has nice leathery leaves and bell-shaped, dark pink, or pink and white flowers. It is about 10cm (3in) tall, and of course requires acid, moist soil. The fruit is edible and is used for jam and in drinks.

Following pages: Saxifrages are very versatile.

Pinus leucodermis *'Schmidtii' is a witche's broom form, and an excellent choice for the rock garden.*

Conifers Conifers also deserve a space in a book about rock plants. At the mention of conifers, you may immediately think of the much too tall *Chamaecyparis* 'Leylandii' that grows in the neighbour's garden and blocks the light to your windows. These are not quite the conifers I had in mind. There are now a large number of dwarf conifers available which make a framework for the rock garden and provide colour in winter.

There are different small cultivars of *Abies* available which can be planted in the rock garden.

Abies balsamea 'Nana' has a low, rounded growth pattern with short, dark green needles.

From *A. concolor*, the cultivar 'Gable's Weeping' is remarkable for its very slow growth. A. koreana 'Silber Kugel', a cultivar of the Korean fir, is a conifer with a spherical form, and *A. lasiocarpa* 'Compacta', the subalpine fir, is a compact, conical dwarf cultivar with short, blue-grey needles.

Chamaecyparis lawsoniana 'Forsteckensis', a member of the cypress family, has woolly branches and scales.

Chamaecyparis lawsoniana 'Minima Glauca' is a spherical shrub with bluish-green foliage. *C. obtusa* 'Nana Gracilis' is a compact grower with fresh green foliage.

Daphne petraea *'Grandiflora' is a stunning shrub for a container or trough.*

In winter *Cryptomeria japonica* 'Bandai-Sugi' is bronze-coloured. It is sensitive to frost. *Cryptomeria japonica* 'Vilmoriniana' grows very slowly. The needles turn brown during the winter.

Juniperus communis 'Compressa' grows into a splendid, low, compact pillar, while *Juniperus media* 'Old Gold' is broad and squat. There is also the attractive, blue-grey *J. squamata* 'Blue Star'.

The *Larix* or larch has the pretty cultivar, *Larix decidua* 'Vasikov', which grows into a witche's broom shape. This is a lovely Czech cultivar for the rock garden.

There is a beautiful example of *Microbiota decussata* in the arboretum at Trompenburg. It is an easily pruned conifer which turns brown in winter.

There are a number of forms of *Picea abies*, the Norway spruce, which are suitable for the rock garden.
Picea abies 'Acrocona' and *P.a.* 'Acrocona Nana' are already decorated with beautiful red cones when they are still quite young.
P.a. 'Little Gem' is also suitable for the rock garden with its short, bright green needles. *P.g.* 'Echiniformis' is spherical with blue-grey needles.

A framework of conifers is not only functional in winter; the evergreen foliage also serves as a peaceful contrast to the colourful rock plants.

Pinus mugo 'Mops' is a tightly-packed, dwarf variety and *Pinus mugo* 'Ophir' has pale green needles which turn a remarkable yellow colour in winter. *P. parviflora* 'Adcock's Dwarf' is another cultivar that deserves consideration for the small rock garden.

During the winter this conifer (Larix kaempferi) *has a beautiful silhouette.*

Pseudotsuga menziesii 'Little Jamie' has a lovely globe shape and grows very slowly.

Taxus baccata 'Green Column' is a wonderful yew for the rock garden because its growth is so restricted.

Finally, I want to mention *Tsuga canadensis* 'Cole's Prostrate', which extends very slowly.

Propagation

In this chapter I will discuss the various methods of propagation, such as sowing, dividing, rooting cuttings, and layering. Since I am only concerned with methods of propagation I have not included plant names.

Potentilla 'Goldrush' is a hybrid that sometimes flowers twice in one year if the autumn is wet.

Since so many different plants are grown in a rock garden, it is virtually impossible to discuss the propagation of every individual plant in detail.

I have already mentioned the best method of propagation for the plants or trees in question: Chapter 4 is about suitable plants, Chapter 5 is about bulbs and tubers in the rock garden, and Chapter 6 is about trees and shrubs.

Growing from seed

The first method of propagation is obviously sowing. As a rule, a flowering plant produces fruit in which the seeds are stored. Depending on the species, these seeds can be sown when they are fresh or ripe. Before sowing you need a good, fine, sterile compost, that is free of any harmful organisms. You can buy ready-prepared compost at a nursery or reputable garden centre. Normal sand, which also has to be clean, can also be used. I often use silver sand or the finer river sand. Use some fine gravel for better drainage in pots and containers. You can usually find this at pet shops or garden centres specializing in ponds and aquaria.

Use clean pots, bowls, seed-trays or seed-beds to sow the seeds.

Plastic pots and old-fashioned clay pots are suitable for this.

The advantages of plastic pots are that they are easily cleaned, and, because they do not have porous sides, no disease germs are left behind.

Following pages:
Pulsatilla vernalis *thrives in dry ground.*

123

They do not have to be soaked in water before use, because they do not absorb water. They are better insulated and do not dry out as quickly as earthenware pots. There is also a disadvantage: if you tend to over-water, the seedlings can rot. In addition, you need labels in order to know what plants you have sown; relying on your memory is just not good enough. I have seen too many mistakes made that way. It is also advisable to keep some kind of diary to record which plants you have sown and the exact date.

There are lists which give the number of days each plant will need to germinate.

You do not have to follow this slavishly, because the conditions under which you plant the seeds are also an important factor, but a list will give you a good indication.

When you have made the necessary preparations you can start sowing. You start with a thin layer of gravel at the bottom of the pot, on top of which you put the compost and sand. The pots, trays, and dishes, or whatever containers you are using, are filled to approximately 1cm (1/2in) below the rim. This makes it easy for you to water the plants and prevent the seeds washing away in the rain if you sink these pots in the ground out of doors.

The seeds should be well spread out in the container, because when the seedlings sprout they need sufficient space to start growing.

Erigeron aureus *can be grown from seed.* You need to cover the seeds with compost, the depth depending on

their size. Give very fine seeds just a quick watering with a fine-spray-ed watering-can. Cover large seeds with a layer of soil as deep as the seeds themselves. Use the same seed compost, but seive it first.

This compost has to be dry, otherwise the seed cannot germinate because the compost is too heavy and tightly packed. You can also cover the seeds with very fine gravel, but only do this when you know the seeds take more than one or two weeks to germinate. With gravel, the upper layer of soil will not dry out so easily and the seeds will germinate better. After sowing, you must check the humidity of the pots regularly.

If they are not sufficiently damp you can give them extra water using the fine rose on the watering-can. If the plants are outside and the weather is particularly cold, you should cover them with horticultural fleece. In case of persistent rainfall, it is recommended that you move the pots inside or place them in a container or frame. If not there is the risk that all your sowing efforts will be in vain and you will only find that the seeds have rotted in the pots. As soon as the plants have shoots of a reasonable size you can prick them out.

Take a rather larger pot or seed tray and position the plants so that they have plenty of space. When I am pricking out I always work with two wooden spatulas. I make a notch in one of them. Then I use the straight one to lift the plants out of the compost and I use the one with the notch to hold the plants.

Saxifraga stolitzkae *can be propagated by rooting the individual rosettes.*

Fritillaria davisii *is a species of* Fritillaria *that only grows to 20cm (8in).*

Once you have made a hole in the compost you can just slide the plant in. You now press the compost firmly around the seedling so that its roots are in contact with the compost and there is no chance that they will dry out.

Now the seedlings can start developing a substantial clump of roots.

If the seeds have still not germinated after a reasonable length of time and frequent checking on your part, it is possible that these seeds will only germinate after a cold period. You can leave these particular seeds outside for another winter and if nothing appears after a year or two you can throw the seeds away.

Gentiana verna *can also be grown from seed.*

Division   Division, also called splitting up, is a very simple method of propagation. You do this by lifting the plant from the ground and tearing or cutting it apart. Naturally, you must make sure that each separate piece has its own roots.

For plants with single roots this method is unsuccessful.

These plants have one long root, while other plants produce a clump of roots.

Plants with single roots are not so easy to transplant. As with any method of planting, splitting up is best done in the spring and autumn.

Plants that flower in early spring can still be divided after flowering, but if they flower in late spring, it is better to wait until the autumn.

If you divide them too late, there is a risk that they will not take properly before the first frosts, and will die.

Divided plants are normally transplanted straight away, but if you are anxious that you may lose the plant for some reason, you can plant the pieces in pots initially and wait for them to become properly established.

Plants such as *Aubrieta*, *Arabis*, *Haberlea*, *Veronica*, and many other species are easy to propagate by division.

Cuttings   Another form of vegetative propagation is by taking cuttings. Here you need a special compost for cuttings that can be made up in various ways. Everyone has their own method for making up compost for cuttings, but it usually consists of sand and peat.

Two parts of coarse sand and one part of peat make a satisfactory, light mixture. You fill the pot or container for the cuttings with this mixture. Cover the container with a sheet of glass or put a plastic bag on top of the pot and put it in a warm place, but not directly in the sun.

Small propagators are ideal for this purpose. These consist of two plastic boxes, one of which is transparent and allows light through. This is used to cover the cuttings.

If the cuttings are covered, the compost stays humid and a high air humidity is maintained, so that they have a better chance of taking.

Thymus serpyllum, *shown here with* Helichrysum, *can be propagated from cuttings.*

The compost in which cuttings are set must always be pressed down firmly. There are hormone rooting powders or solutions that encourage the cuttings to grow.

One of those products is Jiffygrow solution. For cuttings that root with difficulty, it might be worth considering using a product like that, but I must add that there are plants for which it either does not work or has a negative effect. It is better to experiment beforehand, but of course you do not have to start from scratch.

Experienced gardeners will no doubt be only too happy to give you advice.

Stem cuttings

You can take stem cuttings either immediately after flowering or in October to November. The first cuttings are called summer cuttings, and the later ones winter cuttings. Generally shoot cuttings are taken from plants which seed with difficulty or not at all, from plants which will not breed true from seed, and also from plants that do not split very well naturally.

As already mentioned, you take summer cuttings directly after flowering, which is usually in July or August.

The shoots are then firm enough, but not too stiff. Take the cutting with a sharp knife and remove the lowest leaves. Make an oblique cut just below a leaf bud and, if you wish, dip it in a rooting powder or solution.

It is possible to construct a beautiful rock garden in a flat landscape.

Shake the cutting to remove the surplus, because there should not be surplus powder or solution left on the cutting. Then place the cutting in the compost and cover the pot or container with a sheet of glass or plastic.

Ferns, shown here in the gardens of the University of Utrecht, like acid soil.

Autumn cuttings

Autumn cuttings are placed in a cold-frame or greenhouse and covered with a mat of reeds or a screen. In frost-free weather, you can remove the cover and the tray will be ventilated. Usually the cuttings will have rooted during the winter.

Shoot cuttings or buds

Shoot cuttings or buds are cuttings taken early in the year from the growing parts of the plant. These cuttings are made at an angle just below the leaf bud. In this case you also remove the lowest leaves otherwise they will rot in the cutting compost. Shoot cuttings or buds are then handled in the same way as stem cuttings.

Cuttings with a heel

With a few plants, particularly woody varieties, it is preferable to use an older piece of the plant's wood. Woody cuttings are usually taken from firm, one-year old twigs, but cuttings from two- or three-year-old ones can also give good results.

To obtain a heel, the cuttings are torn from the plant. In this way, a piece of older wood comes away with the torn-off twig or branch.

In order to make sure that this heel does not decay in the growing

medium, you must trim it. Make a small hole in the compost and place the cutting in it. This method of cutting is especially used with plants that are difficult to propagate even with a rooting medium under a plastic cover.

Rhododendron ferrugineum *is native to alpine meadows.*

Leaf cuttings

Although not many rock plants can be propagated by leaf cuttings, it is the best method of propagation with, for example, *Ramonda* and *Haberlea*.

You remove a leaf with the stem attached and place it in the cutting compost stalk down to a depth of 2cm (1in).

The leaf must have a bud in the leaf axil. It takes rather a long time before the cuttings form roots and shoots, but I always think this is a spectacular way of producing new plants.

Root cuttings

A few other rock plants can be propagated by means of a root cutting. This is a very simple method of propagation. In the spring, completely remove the plant from the ground, cut off the thicker pieces of root and use these for propagation.

Cut them into small pieces – straight across the top and angled at the bottom.

Put them in a container with the compost used for cuttings and cover them with moist sand.

Put this container in a warm place and keep everything damp.

In the course of time you will discover that the root cuttings have formed buds, and then the shoots will appear.

Plants which are propagated by this method include *Erodium*, some varieties of *Geranium*, *Mertensia*, *Morisia monanthos*, *Primula denticulata*, and *Pulsatilla vulgaris*.

Layering   Finally I want to mention layering. Woody plants are often propagated in this way. Bend a branch down to the ground and keep it in contact with the soil with the help of a stone. In time the branch forms roots underneath the stone. You can separate this plant from the parent and plant it somewhere else.

This is a reliable method of propagation because you only remove the new plant from the parent when it has formed roots.

Aster alpinus *'Albus'*
creates a very pleasing
effect in the rock
garden.

This beautiful
Acantholimon albanicum
loves the sun.

Maintenance

As you may have noticed, every type of garden requires some sort of maintenance. Whether it is a border with hardy perennials, a rock garden, a trough, or a scree slope, one thing is certain, and that is there is work to be done.

A rock garden requires lot of maintenance because the weeds that become established between the plants will have to be removed by hand. Use a knife to remove the weeds, including those with a tap root.

In addition, use a small hand-rake, which actually looks more like a fork, to aerate the ground again.

Winter maintenance

Winter is the ideal season to change or improve parts of your garden if you so wish.

When the weather is too wet you can cover the outdoor plants in your rock garden with a sheet of glass.

The hairy plants are especially sensitive to the damp that is such a feature of the winter in western Europe. As you have read earlier in this book, most rock plants appreciate a blanket of snow, but conifers and evergreen shrubs, just like border plants, do not benefit from such a heavy covering of snow, so just tap the snow off those shrubs and they will be undamaged.

Spring maintenance

In spring there are other jobs to bear in mind. For example, how are the birds and slugs faring in your garden. If they are eating your plants you should plan some kind of protection.

You can catch the slugs in a jar filled with beer and then sunk to the rim in the soil, and you can protect the plants from birds with some

netting. Fortunately, birds do not attack all plants, so keeping them away should not be a huge task.

Even an alpine house requires maintenance.

It is necessary to remove the sheets of glass from delicate plants as soon as they start growing.

Do not celebrate the arrival of spring too soon, because a late frost can cause a lot of damage.

Listen carefully to the weather forecasts in case a frost is expected, so that you can cover the plants that already have tender new growth.

Of course, you will inspect your garden in order to see which plants have not survived the winter.

Perhaps you did not put the plant in the right spot, or it may be that planting too close together has had unfortunate consequences.

Try to grow it in another spot, but be sure to remove all traces of the disaster.

Summer maintenance   In summer the rock garden is a sea of colour. Clear up the spring flowers which are over, collect seeds, remove yellowing leaves, and check the plants for disease or pests. In a dry period it is also important to give them enough water. In addition, you can start to propagate plants from cuttings.

Pests and Diseases   Pests and diseases is not a particularly pleasant topic but unfortunately it is one that cannot be avoided, even in a rock garden.

Cabbage white butterflies love Phlox.

Diseases   A plant that is not growing well will be affected sooner than one in perfect condition.

In this case, I am thinking of fungal infections in particular, which occur in plants that have difficulties with our damp winters.

There are remedies for fungi, but the secret is to catch them in time. Moulds and fungi spread in damp periods by transferring their spores from plant to plant, and before you know it, a whole group of plants are affected.

Pests   Pests are the destroyers of gardens. One of the most annoying pests is the slug, which is capable of stripping a whole plant bare on its own. You can destroy these in two ways.

You can use slug pellets that are scattered between the plants, but I prefer not to use them. I would rather see natural predators such as birds, toads, and hedgehogs, eat these pests.

However, in a wet year there can be so many slugs that there are not enough predators to keep them under control. As far as possible, I try to catch as many slugs as I can by using jars filled with beer, in which the slugs drown.

Birds can also be annoying because they disturb the ground in their search for food, to make sure that there are different kinds of fruits and berries in the garden so that the birds do not have to hunt for food in the rock garden.

Another problem is the butterfly, which can look so attractive but can do so much damage. It lays its eggs on the underside of the leaves of its food plants and after the larvae hatch they will eat the whole plant in no time.

Early in the season, the cabbage white and brimstone butterflies are searching for *Phlox* and *Aubrieta* to begin their attack on your garden. As soon as I spot butterflies, I look around the garden to see if there are already any eggs on the underside of the leaves.

I remove the leaves concerned from the plant.

In this way I have butterflies in my garden but fewer threadbare plants. The hawk moth, which likes carnations, is another insect capable of doing considerable damage.

Aphids can also be active in the rock garden. Only a few plants are prone to attack by them, and because in many cases you will have only one plant from each species in your garden, the infestation will be limited to that particular plant.

As soon as that plant is covered in aphids it no longer looks attractive and besides, the insects are sapping the plant's strength.

You should therefore do something about it at the first sign of aphids. A little detergent in water is quite effective for removing aphids es-

Slugs adore campanulas. The photograph shows Campanula formanekiana.

Make sure that the troughs do not dry out.

A choice of troughs, a delight to the eye.

pecially if you use a spray. You could also use a soapy cloth to wipe them off, or a paint brush on delicate plants.

There are systemic insecticides available which kill insects via the plant tissues.

Small mammals   Moles are beautiful and useful animals because they eat the insects that plague your plants, but as in any type of garden, they can be very annoying in a rock garden. They tunnel underground and then throw up heaps of earth.

Catching a mole is not simple. Mole traps are cruel. You can also lay in wait for the animals early in the morning with a spade.

There are all kinds of myths about scaring moles, but none of these methods seem to be very successful. I always say that it is a pleasure to have moles because at least this means that you have a garden and that it is quite rural.

As well as troublesome insects there are some that are a delight to have in a garden. Think of bees, for example.

It is a magnificent sight to see them collecting nectar from flowers in the garden and at the same time assisting the gardener by pollinating plants.

Sedum, Salvia, Cotoneaster, and many other plants will ensure that these insects continue to visit the rock garden.

Useful addresses

**Rock Gardens to visit
(by country, in alphabetical order)**

Botanic Gardens
University of British Columbia
Vancouver
British Columbia
Canada

**Jardin Botanique de Montréal
(Montreal Botanic Garden)**
4101 rue Sherbrooke Est
Montréal (Québec)
Canada

National Botanic Garden
Glasnevin
Dublin
Eire

Royal Botanic Garden
Exhibition Road
Kew
London
England

RHS Garden, Wisley
Wisley, Woking
Surrey
England

Royal Botanic Garden, Edinburgh
Edinburgh
Midlothian
Scotland

**Botanic Garden, University
of Utrecht**
Fort Hoofddijk
Budapestlaan 17
de Uithof
Utrecht
The Netherlands

The Arnold Arboretum
Jamaica Plain
Massachusetts
USA

Betty Ford Alpine Gardens
Ford Park
Vail
Colorado
USA

Brooklyn Botanic Garden
1000 Washington Avenue
Brooklyn
NY11225
USA

**The Huntingdon Botanical
Gardens**
San Marino
California
USA

The New York Botanical Garden
Bronx
New York
USA

Societies

**Vancouver Island Rock and Alpine
Garden Society**
Box 6507
Victoria
British Columbia V8P 5M4
Canada

The Royal Horticultural Society
80 Vincent Square
London SW1P 2PE
England

Alpine Garden Society
E.M. Upward
The AGS Centre
Avonbank
Pershore
Worcs WR10 3JP
England

Scottish Rock Garden Club
Dr I Boyd
Groom's Cottage
Kirklands
Ancrum
Jedburgh TD8 6UJ
Scotland

Dutch Rock Garden Society
Sec. A. Musch
Bovenkamp 3
3985 PH Werkhoven
The Netherlands

**North American Rock Garden
Society**
Executive Secretary NARGS
PO Box 67
Millwood
NewYork 10546
USA

Photo credits

G.W.M. Borgonje, Raalte: title page, pp. 6, 9, 10, 11, 12-13, 14, 15, 16 left, 17, 18, 19, 20, 21 top, 22, 23, 25, 26, 27, 28, 29, 30, 31, 32, 33 bottom, 34-35, 36, 37, 38, 39, 40, 41, 42, 43, 44 right, 45, 46, 47, 48, 49, 50, 51, 52-53, 54, 55, 56-57, 58, 59, 60, 61, 62, 63, 64, 65, 66, 67, 68, 69, 70, 71, 72, 73, 74, 75, 76, 77, 78, 79, 80, 81, 82, 83, 84, 85, 86, 87, 88, 89, 90, 91 right, 92, 93, 94, 95, 96, 97, 98, 99, 100-101, 102, 103, 104, 105, 106, 107, 108, 109, 110, 111, 112, 113, 114, 116, 117, 120, 121, 122, 123, 124-125, 126, 127, 128, 129, 130, 133, 134, 135, 136, 137, 138, 141

M. Kurpershoek, Amsterdam: pp. 8, 16 right, 44 left, 91 left, 118, 119, 131

G. Otter, IJsselstein: pp. 24, 33 top, 115, 132

P. Schut, Haarlem: p. 21 bottom

*You cannot write a book single-handed. That is why I wish
to thank the people mentioned below, who have helped me
in the preparation of this book:
Mr G. Borgonje from Raalte, Mrs F. Dresen-Hoogvelt,
Mrs T. Smits from Waspik, Dr J.W.J. Baron van Till from Rhenen,
and Dr Sir E.G. van Wijhe from Rhenen..*

Bibliography

The following books are valuable reading for enthusiasts:

Alpines, The Easy way, Elliott, Joe, RHS, A Wisley Handbook
Planning and Planting Rock Gardens, Kelly, J., Ward Lock
Rock and Alpine Gardens, Pavey, J., Apple
Rock Gardening, Lowe, D., RHS
Rock Gardening Month by Month, Jefferson-Brown, M.,
   David & Charles
Step-by-Step Ponds, Pools and Rockeries, Swift, P., New Holland
The Rock and Water Garden Expert, Hessayon, D.G., Expert Books

These books have also proved useful in preparing this text:

Rock Garden Plants of North America,
McGary, J., (ed.), Timber Press

The RHS Gardeners Encyclopedia,
Brickhill, C., (ed.), Dorling Kindersley

The RHS Encyclopedia of Gardening,
Brickhill, C., (ed.), Dorling Kindersley

The RHS Plant Finder,
Lloyd, T., (ed.), Moorland Publishing Company Ltd

New Flora of the British Isles,
Stace, C., Cambridge University Press